WISELY, PRAY THE PSALMS

Ambrose Tinsley, OSB

Wisely, Pray The Psalms

A Prayerful Companion to Reading the Psalms

the columba press

First published in 1993 by
the columba press
55A Spruce Avenue, Stillorgan Industrial Park,
Blackrock, Co. Dublin

This edition, 2014

Cover by Bill Bolger
Origination by The Columba Press
Printed in Ireland by SprintPrint Ltd.

ISBN 978 1 78218 170 5

Note

The title of this book comes from a psalm-verse which St Benedict used when speaking in the famous Rule about the saying or the singing of the psalms. The phrase he knew was 'Psallite sapienter' and comes from the Latin (Vulgate) psalter. It could be translated 'sing ye wisely' or 'wisely, sing the psalms' or 'wisely, play the harp and sing the psalms'. The version used today in Roman Catholic liturgy reads 'sing with all your skill'. It can be found in Ps 46/47.

Quotations from the psalms are taken from the Grail translation and are used by permission of A. P. Watt Ltd, London.

CONTENTS

Trinity

PART TWO

*Some verses, mostly taken from the psalms which we
have seen already, but arranged so that they can be
used as guide-words for a personal retreat.*

PART THREE

Introduction

It was suggested to me years ago that I should write a book on Psalms. But what kind of book? I thought about it for a while and then decided that the most important things had probably been said a hundred times and, more deflatingly, that, without special academic training, there was little I could do except, perhaps, give encouragement to people to take up the Psalms and then to read them for themselves.

> I would urge you to spend quite a lot of time looking
> at, mulling over, reading privately the psalms.[1]

Those words of Cardinal Basil Hume, when he was Abbot of the monastery at Ampleforth, sum up quite well the kind of thing which down the years I have not only tried to do myself, but have proposed to others, whether clerical or lay. Indeed I am convinced that it is often quite enough because the Psalms, as many people testify, have their own way of speaking to the human heart and human hearts have their own way of understanding what the psalmist really means and of responding to the One of whom they speak.

And yet I must confess that in myself I found the urge to write this book. It came, to some extent, from the conviction that we all can help each other to discover what the Spirit says (and not just through the psalms, although of course it is the psalms which will concern us here). It came, as well, from the awareness that there are, in fact, so many people who have helped me down the years to value and to pray the psalms and that, if I acknowledge them in general and sometimes by a special reference, they may, through my words now, be able to help other people too. To them this book is definitely due.

It is a book for those who use, or want to use, the psalms in their own private prayer. Some will, perhaps, possess a copy of the Church's Daily Prayer and they may use it, or a part of it, each day. It is with them in mind that when I quote a psalm-verse it is taken from the version which they know, the one known as the Grail translation, which Collins published many years ago. It has, of course, its limitations; the most annoying is no doubt its use of non-inclusive words. I have in places tried to rectify that fault but must in many cases leave that to the reader to do for him or herself.

However, I would hope that what I write will be of value too to those who just dip into their own Bibles and who, therefore, use the psalms in a less structured way. I hope that they will be encouraged by my overall approach and that their love for these old treasured prayers will consequently grow. And, to facilitate them, I have given to each psalm which I have quoted both its number in the Grail edition (and the Prayer Book of the Church) and that which can be found in most of the editions of the Bibles which are sold in shops today.[2] The Bible-number generally is 'one more' than that used in liturgical editions.

But let me also say a word about the structure of this book. The first part is an outline presentation of the psalms and in a three-fold pattern which will become, as the last section shows, the movement of the Trinity itself. The second part builds on the first and offers certain psalms, or verses, which the reader can take up and use for his or her own personal retreat. The third part speaks about the cursing-psalms, about the dignity of those who have been called to share the life of Christ and then about that deep and silent prayer which takes place in the heart and which becomes a witness to the Spirit dwelling there and to the fact that we are, somehow, in that 'unifying Trinity' itself! As for the Notes, let me just say that, while they should be useful to those readers who have at their side a Bible or a Psalter, they contain as well a number of important points which should be in the text itself but could not find a place. And so they too, I would suggest, are worthy of attention.

And so, to come back to our basic theme, I pray that as we celebrate the words which we discover in the psalms we will be guided by the Spirit to become ourselves 'a word', a word which echoes Christ who is the Word-made-flesh, a word which through him now gives glory to the Father of us all. Amen, so let it be.

Part One

ESSENTIALS

Personalities

There are many people, or rather types of people, who reveal themselves to us when we sit down and quietly read through the psalms. Some lines indeed, when we reflect on them, appear quite clearly to be spoken by a different person than the ones which went before and those which come immediately after often seem to be the words of someone else. Of course there are no captions indicating who says this or that, as there would be in, let us say, an ordinary play, and so we have to learn how to supply this information for ourselves. I will give some examples in a moment of the kind of people whom we will discover but allow me first to say that, if we want to find the different characters, the lines may have to be divided in a way which does not correspond to the divisions in the printed text nor to the way the psalms are often sung. There is another rhythm, we might call it a dramatic rhythm, in the text and it can often be for us rewarding to discover what it is.

The personalities, whom we will find when we begin to look for them, will certainly include such people as 'the Pilgrim' who is travelling, or who wants to travel, to some holy place. They will include 'the Scholar' too, by which I simply mean the one who likes to read the sacred books and then to ponder carefully the message they contain. And then there may appear to us 'the Wise Man' or 'the Sage', that is the one who, from the wealth of his experience, desires to share with other people insights about life which he himself has managed to acquire. And after that 'the Prophet', who consoles or even warns the people whom he meets, may make his presence felt. And finally there is 'the King', that dominating figure who lived in Jerusalem and who from there, at least implicitly, directed the activity of all. We could go on. Indeed one fairly recent author made a list of thirty personalities[1] but let me settle, for the most part, for these special and important five.

However, we must admit that these personalities lived a long time ago. And yet it can be said that they are also accessible today. Indeed, and this is most important for our own use of the psalms, these personalities whom I have mentioned here are in each one of us as well! They may not be so, I agree, in a developed or much less a perfect way but they are there, and what is more they all with some encouragement can grow. And so as we reflect upon the psalms we can discover in ourselves some elements of all these five and even come to realise that we, to some extent, are they!

We can indeed say that we are to some extent 'the pilgrim' now for every day we grope with more or less success towards the happiness we seek. But, if we do, it must be also said that we can know more clearly than the psalmist ever did that happiness cannot be fully found at any earthly shrine but only in the New Jerusalem above.

We are 'the scholar', too, or can be when we sit down with the sacred books and ponder what they say. This 'personality', which should not here be understood in any over-academic sense, is often very undeveloped and especially perhaps today for we are living in a world which gives us little opportunity for quiet personal reflection. But, if we make room for it and foster it, it can become, as many people whom I know will testify, a powerful and a beneficial influence within our daily lives.

We are 'the sage', 'the wise one', when enriched by our own personal experience of life and by the wisdom we absorb from others we discover that we know what should be done and realise that we are able to help others understand the art of living too.

We are the 'prophet' when, from an awareness of the world we cannot see and from a strong conviction that the God who made us is a God of love, we help those whom we meet to find his presence for themselves and then, with confidence, to put their trust in him.

We are the king! In olden times he was of course a person of great power. He fought the enemies of his dominion and he was expected to make laws so that all those who lived within it could do so in peace. Our territory is of course a less extensive one! It is in many cases just our very selves. Yet within it there can be 'enemies' which have to be repelled and there remains a need for rules and regulations so that every part of us, at least all the essential ones, can grow. And so there has to be a 'king' in us to regulate our often complicated lives!

I have, I know, been moving here from saying that these 'personalities' in some way are in us to saying that we are ourselves those very 'personalities'. But both in different ways are true. The second statement, that we are those 'personalities', is true especially when we have activated in ourselves the 'personality' concerned and, therefore, for a little while identify with it. The first, however, namely that we have this 'personality' or that within us, seems to say that it may not yet be completely developed and also that there may be other 'personalities' in us as well. Indeed there has to be if only for the reason that one by itself and without any help from others cannot fully grow. The 'king' in us, to give an obvious example, needs the help of 'people' like the 'scholar' and the 'sage' if it is to develop well, and they in turn, if they are to grow properly, require the space and the encouragement which only one with royal power can guarantee. As for the pilgrim, as we will discover in the psalms themselves, he also has to go to someone else if he desires to get the help and the direction that he needs.

Movements of the heart

What the psalms express, however, are the movements of the heart. They are themselves, as we have seen, the words of people like the prophet and the pilgrim but what they reveal is how those people actually felt and how they then reacted to the God on whom all situations, ultimately, must depend. And so, as we read through the psalms today, we can discover people who were happy and whose happiness, indeed, could often bubble into praise. And we can find some people who were sad, annoyed, angry or frustrated because life did not go the way they wanted. But in them all we find as well an underlying and a strong conviction that, although he may seem absent, God exists and that he can, and will in some way, solve all problems and fulfil the promises which he has made.

The 'movements of the heart' which are expressed in these long-treasured psalms occur, however, in ourselves as well. The early Fathers of the Church were quite aware of that and one of them in fact, in writing to a friend, refers to psalms as 'mirrors' in which those, who use them, can see something of themselves.

> It seems to me that these words become like a mirror to the person singing them so that he might perceive himself and the emotions of his soul,[2]

he wrote. Indeed to read the psalms, and even Scripture as a whole, as if it were a 'mirror' is to follow in the steps of many who, it seems, were taught to do the same. Today, of course, such an approach can have a very strong appeal. Today, especially, a lot of people tend to be more interested in who they are and in their own particular journey through this life than they are in the lives of others who lived long ago. And so, if they sit down and read the psalms which were composed by people in the past, they like to understand them in relation to the needs which they themselves experience and to the mystery of their own unfolding lives.

A good example would be how we tend to use psalm 22/23, the so-called 'Shepherd Psalm'. In it we listen to the words of someone who has learnt to put his trust in God and who is, consequently, happy in himself.

> The Lord is my shepherd;
> there is nothing I shall want,[3]

he says and in the lines which follow that same note of content-ment keeps on coming through.

> If I should walk in the valley of darkness
> no evil would I fear.[4]

Such a person we can easily admire. Such a person we can even envy! Yet the confidence and trust which we admire and envy in the psalmist must, to some extent, be in ourselves as well!

It may not be too strong a quality and it may seem at times to disappear but it is surely there. Indeed, as we allow the words of this most popular of psalms to echo in our hearts, we can at times not only feel that this capacity to trust is somehow struggling in ourselves but that it is, in some way, actually growing. And, when that occurs, we may become aware that this new confidence is coming, not just from ourselves, but from another power which is within us and which, fortunately, is much stronger than our own!

Let me recall in this connection an experience which I had many years ago. It was when in Nigeria a young nurse told me that each day, before she went down to the wards, she said, as her own special prayer, a certain verse of what is not, perhaps, the best-known of the psalms. It was the verse which, as we have it, reads

Give success to the work of our hands.[5]

I was, I can remember, fascinated at the time because her comment offered me a new and quite exciting application of a verse which I had known but which, in fact, I had not thought about too much till then. It was, moreover, one which could, I knew as well, be taken up and used in different ways by other people too. But what impressed me most was the simplicity with which that young nurse could reveal to me a detail of her life which was quite obviously intimate. She said it in a way which seemed to say, to me at least, that, though it was itself a simple thing, it came from somewhere deep within, from her own 'heart' or from her 'spirit', if you would prefer that word.

From her spirit! But, as soon as we say that, we have to think as well about that other Spirit which, according to St Paul, is mingling with our own.[6] It is the Spirit which comes down from God and which desires to bring us all to him. It is the Spirit which was in the psalmists in the past and which now helps each one of us when we try to discover, as that young nurse did, a meaning in their words which we can make our own. It is the Spirit which can lead us then into that silence where, beyond all human words and even thoughts, we can be one with him who is Infinity itself.

God

The name most often used for God by those whom we meet in the psalms is 'Lord'. But 'Lord' is the translation of a Hebrew word (Yahweh) which was, the Scriptures say, revealed to Moses at the burning bush.[7] It was a word which, at the time, suggested that God wanted to release the people, who had been enslaved, and then to bring them to a 'Promised Land'. But it suggested, too, a God of awe-inspiring greatness, and, indeed, a greatness which, perhaps, can only be appreciated by those people who, like Moses, know the unrelenting vastness of the desert. Moses hid his face![8] He could not look on God! He could, in no way, treat him as an equal or as somebody with whom He could attempt to bargain. He could only worship and then do whatever was required!

The followers of Moses down the ages worshipped Yahweh too. Even when they left the desert and began to settle in a land which they would call their own they did not lose their spiritual contact with that mighty presence in their midst although, as we are told, some did succumb to the temptation to accept the popular and much more manageable gods which other peoples had. But on the whole, thanks to succeeding prophets, their commitment to the Lord who had delivered them remained and was transmitted from one generation to the next. And so the people went to different local shrines to give thanks to the Lord but later on the custom grew of travelling to the temple at Jerusalem itself. And there, as we can see by carefully reading the psalms, the leaders of the temple liturgies encouraged all from time to time with phrases such as these:

Bow down before his holy mountain
for the Lord, our God, is holy[9]

and

Come in; let us bow and bend low
let us kneel before the God who made us.[10]

Kneel, bow down, bend low! And that, no doubt, is what they did, those people who had gathered there. They worshipped with their bodies and not only with their souls!

Today we have that same religious need although it has, as we all know, been somewhat stifled by our western society today. And yet it can, as we know too, begin to reassert itself at times, as when we see a range of mighty mountains or the wildness of the sea! Or it can make itself felt when a 'miracle' takes place: the unexpected resolution of a problem or the healing of some sickness or disease. And then, as somebody once said to me, you know there is 'a man above' and somewhere in ourselves we bow and give him thanks and maybe wonder how it is that we, who know that we do not deserve it, could have been so blessed! And if at such a moment someone were to say

The Lord is great, highly to be praised[11]

we would agree and maybe even seek a church where we could praise him publicly!

I must say something more about the Spirit here because it is that Spirit (which is mingling with our own) that moves us when we give such thanks and praise. And so we find that when we pray it is not just a dialogue between God and ourselves but the activity of three: ourselves and God and his dynamic and involving Spirit. And, indeed, because that Spirit, which is in us, is, and was, in others too and not least in the second and the greater Moses, Jesus, we can say that it is also 'with all those and him', that we now pray to God. But we can also go a little further here for Jesus was, as we all know, a very special person and, according to liturgical tradition, has a very special place in this activity of prayer. And so we can say now that it is not just 'with him' but 'through him' as well that our prayer is received. Our prayer! It is indeed our own but then, through Christ and in the Spirit, it is also part of something which is greater, much greater, too.

The first time I became explicitly aware of this invisible dimension in our praying of the psalms was probably when, as a young monk, I was visiting the secondary school where I had been. I met, while walking down the corridors, a priest whom I had known quite well and who, although he welcomed me sincerely, was quite obviously taken by surprise. He said, quite suddenly and unexpectedly, that it was such a pity that the psalms contained no reference at all to those essential articles of faith: the Incarnation and the Trinity! I think he felt that psalms would be a suitable and edifying topic for a person such as me! In any case I felt, instinctively, that what he said was wrong although, perhaps quite fortunately, I could not say then exactly why. But now I think I know. It is because he did not see that, since the psalms are prayers of people who possess the same humanity as Christ and since they are inspired by that same Spirit which was his, they must in some way be his prayers as well. And so the Incarnation is implied in every one! And since the psalms are prayers of Christ, the whole Christ we could say, they ultimately come from that same Holy Spirit and are offered to the Father who accepts them all. And so the Trinity itself is also celebrated there!

Indeed it could be argued that there is no need at all to add the 'Glory be' at the conclusion of each psalm for each psalm is itself an act of praise to God. My priestly friend suggested that the 'Glory be' was the salvation of the psalm for it supplied, he said, what was for him so obviously lacking in the sacred text but that, as we have seen, is really not the case. It would of course be better if the 'Glory be', which is in fact appended to the singing of most psalms, was not the present but the older one,[12] the one which offered glory, not to all three persons of the Trinity, but to the Father, *through* the Son and *in* the Holy Spirit. Such a formula, unlike the later anti-Arian revision which we have,[13] would much more accurately emphasise the true dynamic of the psalm itself. And it might also help to make us more aware that we ourselves are not just, as it were, outside the triune life of God but, somehow, called to be, and grow, within it, too!

PEOPLE

Introduction

This chapter is about those people who, as I have mentioned, speak in many of the psalms. They are, though not exclusively, the Pilgrim and the Scholar and the Sage, the Prophet and the King. But if we spend some time reflecting now on each of these five personalities, let us remember that the psalms are the result of a lot of temple-polishing and what may have once recorded some particular event has been transformed so that it can become more meaningful to all. One writer, Albert Gelin, put it thus:

> Psalms express a concrete situation. But if these spontaneous prayers are going to be used in public worship they had to flow in moulds or patterns prepared beforehand. Just as a symphony follows certain laws, so too a psalm conforms to a recognisable style or type.[1]

It is important to acknowledge this liturgical perfecting of the psalms, and indeed the fact that some may have been totally composed for temple use, and we will come back to this factor at a later stage. But, for the moment, let us recognise that it is equally important to recall, as much as this is possible, those 'concrete situations' and the different types of people which were in them. And, this is what we will, now, attempt to do.

The Pilgrim

It was a fairly common practice in Old Testament times for people to set out on pilgrimages. At first the place which most attracted them was probably the little town of Shilo[2] for the Ark itself was guarded there and, as the Israelites believed, it was upon the Ark that Yahweh in a very special manner dwelt. But later, after Shilo

had been desecrated and destroyed, the Ark was brought to Zion
or Jerusalem[3] and, consequently, it was to that city that the people
and the pilgrimages went. And there, to those who gathered in
the temple God appeared to say:

> This is my resting place for ever,
> here have I chosen to live.[4]

And so those people would return, and sometimes even every
year, to give God thanks for all the blessings which they had
received and to petition him for those which, at that moment,
they required.

But much more was demanded than a journey to a shrine. A
pilgrimage implied a spiritual journey too! Indeed, perhaps
because this was not always fully understood, the practice seems
to have commenced of giving those who wanted to set out for
Zion some instruction so that they might undertake the journey
with the proper dispositions and readily receive the blessings
which God actually gives. Those pilgrimage instructions were
most probably the ten commandments, which of course is what
the people of the covenant had promised to obey, or some
restatement of what some of them implied and which would have
been relevant to the temptations of the time. One such, indeed,
may have been that which is contained in psalm fourteen (or
fifteen in the Hebrew Bible) and which seems to be the answer
given to some conscientious pilgrim who, in fact, was looking for
advice. He had enquired:

> Lord, who shall be admitted to your tent
> and dwell on your holy mountain?[5]

And God, presumably through someone like a local Rabbi or a
teaching Levite, told him what he had to do if he was to
successfully complete the journey which he was about to undertake.

Today we might be more inclined to say that we are going, not
to Zion or Jerusalem, but to the New Jerusalem above. Life is
itself, wherever we may be, a journey to another world and that

in fact has been, as we well know, the firm belief of many people down the centuries. I can, to give but one example, quote St Hilary, that not-too-well remembered Bishop of the early church in Gaul. He wrote, as I discovered, in his commentary on this same appealing psalm:

> This prayer is that of one who prays to the Lord and desires to know what virtues, what zeal, what will he ought to have to dwell with God and to rest in his heights and in his heavens.[6]

The reply which we find in the psalm, or some of it, may be of help to us today. But on the other hand we may feel that we have to ask again, and even frequently, the kind of question which the psalmist asked if we are to discover what in our own special situation we must do in order to succeed and to attain those beckoning and somewhat dizzy heights.

And yet while we are moving towards the Holy Place, that New Jerusalem above, there are those other special places which some people sometimes visit on the way. They are those places such as Lourdes, Walsingham and Knock where we are able to receive a grace which in some way anticipates the final ecstasy which will one day, we hope, be ours. Indeed I can remember well that feeling of excitement which I felt myself when, from the window of a train, I had my first glimpse of the skyline of that famous city where the bones of the apostles had been laid to rest and which, I knew, had welcomed pilgrims ever since. And then, a little later, I was there! I felt, perhaps, as did the pilgrim in the psalm who with enthusiasm sang:

> I rejoiced when I heard them say
> 'Let us go to God's house.'
> And now our feet are standing
> within your gates, O Jerusalem.[7]

And yet, of course, that moment of excitement was no more than one brief foretaste of the happiness which we will have at last when we arrive at life's eternally rewarding goal!

The Scholar

Topol, in the film *Fiddler on the Roof,* exclaimed how he would love to do so many things but that 'the most wonderful thing of all would be to read the holy books'. That line caught my attention and I thought of venerable rabbis sitting at their desks and reading in a prayerful way what was for them most certainly the word of God himself. Topol would have liked, he said, to do just that! Of course, as all who saw the film know, he did not show much sign of doing anything about it. But he did have the idea! And the idea he had, or should we call it an ideal, was one which had a long and honoured history of its own. It went back many centuries.

In fact this practice of absorbing holy writ goes back to that day in the reign of king Josiah when somebody in the temple found an unexpected scroll. He read it there and then and when he saw that what it said was urgent, brought it to the secretary to the king who read it too. And then, because the secretary realised that it, indeed, was an important document, he went without delay to see the king himself. The king, the Scriptures tell us, was amazed and not a little startled when he heard what it contained and he decided to convene a meeting of his elders and of all the people too so that they all should hear with their own ears what was for him, so obviously, God's own pleading word. The fascinating story can be found in chapters 22 and 23 of the second Book of Kings and I recall it here, though briefly, for that scroll contained the 'Law' which grew into the Book of Deuteronomy and then became a synonym for all the Bible books which were to be in later years the basic nourishment for those who gave themselves to pondering the word.[8] Indeed that practice was encouraged by the way that future Bible editors touched up the older books so that the heroes of the distant past, although they may in fact have been illiterate themselves, were able to appear as models for the would-be reader of the word![9]

But here we are concerned not just with Bible reading but with where and how this practice is portrayed for us as we read through the psalms. And so let us begin by looking at that psalm which, though it may have been composed outside the temple atmosphere, is now a kind of preface to the psalter as a whole. Its opening verse proclaims:

Happy indeed is the man
… whose delight is the Law of the Lord
and who ponders his Law day and night.[10]

This is a simple statement but it is attractive too and one, moreover, which may hide a thought which could perhaps be useful even in this present age. It is that he who 'ponders' actually 'murmurs' and, in that case, we would have a person who not only reads but reads aloud and the result is that what he is reading he can also hear. Such was the normal practice in the ancient world.

And then, as we continue on, we find another psalmist telling us how good this practice is. It is, he says,

more to be desired than gold,
than the purest of gold
and sweeter … than honey,
than honey from the comb.[11]

And how delectable he makes it seem, this person who not only reads and listens to the word but who in some way actually tastes it too. Indeed I have heard people say that once they get the feel of what the Scriptures say, and here I have slipped in another sense, they have an appetite for more and more and more. The word of God becomes for them alive and very wonderful!

But let me introduce one rather special if long-winded friend. He is the careful persevering author of the psalter's longest psalm.[12] Some people are inclined to say that he is boring and monotonous, which is not altogether false, for he can keep repeating words and he appears to state the same ideas in almost every verse. And yet it would be wrong to simply write him off, for even if his style is unexciting, he himself has a devotion to the word of God which is not unattractive. For example as we read his long and alphabetical production, which in English has, no doubt, lost much of its original appeal, we can find useful verses like:

Your word is a lamp for my steps
and a light for my path[13]

and, a little further on:

The unfolding of your word gives light.[14]

And we, perhaps, begin to see how much this Scripture-loving author may have found the answers to the many problems of his life as he digested and absorbed what obviously was for him a very living word!

Of course this psalmist does take a delight in using words like 'law' and 'precepts' and 'commands' but, if he does, he does not really seem to have what we would call a legalistic mind. He is concerned, no doubt, with rules and regulations but his basic interest is not just to do what is correct but to be close to him whose law it obviously is.

I have sought you with all my heart[15]

he wrote and we get the impression, as we use this psalm, that that indeed is what he must have done. He must have read the word and lived it and, in doing so, found God. And when he thought about the 'promise' which the Lord had made he must have more and more discovered that it was in fact, to some extent at least, already his!

The Sage
The Sage, or Wise-man, had a special place in the unfolding history of the Jewish people which the Bible in its own religious way records. In fact we find him long before the Exodus itself and in the capital of Egypt where he was personified in Joseph who, as we are told, had been a slave but who then managed by his wise decisions to become not only free but very powerful too.[16] And then, but here we jump some centuries, we find the sage personified again, this time in Solomon the king who was, according to tradition and apart from many other things, the author of three thousand proverbs which was how the wisdom of those days was frequently passed on.[17] And then, to take another jump, we can discover in the post-exilic age the evidence

of other sages, though these later ones were influenced not by the practical approach of the Egyptians but by the enquiring and the searching mind of Greece.[18] They asked such questions as 'is there an afterlife at all?' and 'why is it that those who live good lives are those who often have to suffer most?' Of course, they did not find the perfect answer to such questions but, if anything is clear, it is that in each age the Jewish sage belonged to what we might consider as a kind of universal club. And yet his own gift grew, as we shall see, in soil which was quite different to that of all the others and in that soil it developed in a very special way.

But first let us note here a quality which many of the sages had. It was a zeal to pass their wisdom on. They were not, therefore, thinkers living only for themselves, but thinkers who enjoyed a social role and even had some kind of obligation to teach others how to live successfully and why. And so we should not be surprised to hear that Joseph when he was in Egypt was, apart from Organiser of the National Economy, a valued teacher too.

> The ruler of the peoples set him free,
> making him master of his house
> and ruler of all he possessed
> to instruct his princes as he pleased
> and to teach his elders wisdom.[19]

As for king Solomon we could, I'm sure, say much the same for did he not compose those many proverbs and did not the queen of Sheba come to visit him because she heard that he was very wise?[20] Indeed we can imagine him at times surrounded by disciples and declaring to them, in such words as we find in another psalm:

> I will instruct you and teach you
> the way you should go.[21]

That was indeed a sage's way of speaking and, as we can see, some sages must indeed have been among those very people who contributed in different ways to the development and content of the Book of Temple-psalms.

The Jewish and the temple sages were, however, influenced not only by non-Jewish trends, such as the practical approach to life of the Egyptians and the speculations of the Greeks, but by the preaching of the prophets too. They thought and taught within the wider context of their faith and so, while proverbs may at times appear to be completely secular, the meaning of a simple statement such as

turn aside from evil and do good[22]

would certainly have been both given and received in harmony with the official moral teaching of their race. But we can say much more. We can assert that there are statements which, while couched in the didactic language of the sages, introduce ideas which did not come from their experience of ordinary life or from the merely logical considerations of their human minds. A good example would be one which links correct behaviour with the promise of apparently inevitable happiness.

If you trust in the Lord and do good,
you will dwell in the land and be secure[23]

one psalmist sang. And one whom we have seen before, pro-claimed and with conviction that if we obey the Law or Word of God we will most certainly be blessed

like a tree
that is planted beside the flowing waters,
that yields its fruit in due season
and whose leaves will never fail.[24]

A lot of people would of course dismiss such thoughts as utterly naive, for life, as it appears, is not like that at all. The good, who try to do the will of God, do not inevitably prosper while the ones who do are very often those for whom God seems to matter very little. Yet the psalmist, who could not have been so blind as not to see that that is true, knows also that the Lord is good and that he will not leave unaided and without reward all those who put their trust in him. He may not see how that will happen but, with a prophetic insight, he is certain that it will.

There is in this connection one particular psalmist whom we certainly must meet. He is, indeed, a sage but one who ponders on the meaning of this life and on the way it should be lived, not from the standpoint of a Joseph or a Solomon who has great power, but from the level of a person who has very little and who even envies those around him who have so much more than he. He is, however, somebody who knows that, if he were to yield to the temptations which he obviously feels, he would not only violate his conscience but would hurt a lot of other people too. And so we find him saying in his prayer:

> … if I should speak like that
> I should betray the race of your sons.[25]

It is as if he understood that we rely on one another for support much more than many people realise. But he knows something else. He knows that if he is to overcome these worrying temptations and to find some inner peace he will have to discover for himself a source of power which is much greater than his own free will and personal resolve. And so we find this sage, this wise-man, this philosopher of sorts resorting to the temple of the Lord!

> I was always in your presence[26]

he, with some exaggeration, says. But it is there among the faithful in that Holy Place that he becomes convinced again, and no doubt in a deeper way, that in the last analysis God is the most important treasure he can have.

> What else have I in heaven but you?
> Apart from you I want nothing on earth.[27]

he very humbly says. And we, who think about him, realise that he has found another wisdom, one which this world cannot give, a wisdom from above, a wisdom which to many is unknown!

I mention this to show that wisdom in the ordinary sense is never quite enough. It does not bring us to the peace and spiritual happiness which we all need. It is, to use the image of a highway, like an outer lane which goes along so far but which then merges with an inner and ongoing one. This image is perhaps not perfect but it illustrates for us the need we have, while travelling on the 'outer lane', to keep in mind the inner one and to be ready to change over, when we see the sign, so that we may be able to continue on and reach our Promised Land. And yet this image also shows that, while that 'outer lane' is there, it is itself both good and useful and in no way contradicts the movement of the lane which represents our life of faith but goes along with it. Indeed it may suggest as well that, though it may not bring us all the way, it can at times be very good and restful to travel at a slower pace on it and to take time to notice and absorb all that the world around is offering. Then the sage in us will have an opportunity to grow!

The Prophet
Sometimes in the lives of most of us there comes a person who says something which enables us to glimpse a value in ourselves which we perhaps had overlooked or maybe never really known. The sage, or wise-man, in the famous psalm which we have just discussed, may have, in fact, discovered such a person. This is of course a guess for in the psalm itself there is no indication whatsoever that another voice was heard. And yet it must be said that if the psalmist did hear someone speak, someone whom he recogised as speaking on behalf of God, it would explain, to some extent at least, how he, who was so sorely tempted, found the confidence which he was able in the last few verses to express. And so I think it might be quite an interesting, and hopefully useful, exercise to look at other psalms and see if there is any evidence in them to indicate that that in fact is what may have occurred.

And so let us begin by looking at psalm 6 for there the very same phenomenon is found. It is again the psalm of someone who has been distressed and who, this time within the psalm itself, cries out in pleading pain. It is a psalm in which the psalmist then surprises us for, suddenly, he brightens up and says,

> the Lord has heard my weeping
> the Lord has heard my plea.[28]

This is indeed an unexpected change and once again there is no reason given. But again the careful reader may well wonder if whatever happened to console and calm him was not linked in some way to the utterance of someone who was recognised as having at that moment a 'prophetic' power?

And then there is psalm 27/28 which seems to be the pleading of a persecuted man but it too, suddenly and without any warning, changes to become a hymn of grateful praise:

> Blessed be the Lord
> for he has heard my cry[29]

the psalmist sings. But once again we are inclined to ask, 'How did he know? How could he be so sure?' There is no reason given. Yet there is a verse, a few lines further back, which seems to say that it may have been in the Holy Place, within the temple of Jerusalem itself, that what occurred, if anything, took place. And that at least is interesting and maybe even a decisive clue!

So let us pass on to another psalm, a psalm in which some words, which seem to have been said by someone else, are actually heard. It is psalm 54/55, a lamentation of some psalmist who is agitated and upset and yet who can, as we discover, end his prayer with words of confidence and trust. Between those two unequal parts, and so towards the final verse, we hear at last what I shall for the moment call the 'other voice'.

> Entrust your cares to the Lord
> and he will support you[30]

it declares. These are consoling words. They are worthwhile-remembering words. Indeed St Peter in his first epistle quotes them when he wants to calm and to encourage those who find that it is difficult to keep on living Christian lives.[31] And as I found, almost by accident, St Basil used them too when writing to a friend who had been called to take a bishopric but felt unequal to the task![32] And we, of course, could probably discover many reasons for accepting them ourselves. But here the question which we have to ask is who was it who said them in the context of this psalm?

And so let us continue our detective work, this time by moving back to psalm 11/12. There we shall discover what we have been looking for: the final, and until now missing, clue. It is not just that other words are said, or that they are associated with the temple, which in fact is not explicit in this case, but that the one from whom they come is actually mentioned.

'For the poor who are oppressed
and the needy who groan
I myself will arise,'
says the Lord.[33]

They are addressed, we can presume, to him who in the first two verses groaned and cried for help and who is able therefore to conclude the psalm with renewed confidence. And yet of course there is one question still. How did the psalmist know that those much needed words in fact came from the Lord? The answer could be that he knew because they were the kind of words which God had said a hundred times before but it is also very possible, and some would even say 'quite probable', that they were said by someone in the temple who was recognised as being in some very special way the mouthpiece of the Lord.

And so it seems that in the temple there were certain people who possessed this very useful and prophetic gift. They spoke, as we have seen, consoling words and words which tell us that, no matter how depressed we are by what is happening in our lives or even by what we have done ourselves, we need not be afraid. God knows it all and will do all he can to help and set us free!

Be still and know that I am God[34]

he seems, through one of them, to say and that means that there is no problem or distress at all which he cannot resolve and overcome. And so, like many who have heard those words and quietly absorbed them in the past, we now, as we allow them enter into us, can wait with confidence until whatever storm has come will pass or just get up and do, with new-found inner peace, whatever must be done. And then, who knows, some other people may discover that, in some way, we have managed to become 'prophetic people', too!

The King

Kings! They are a less familiar sight today and those we know about are very different to the ones of long ago. In those days they were autocratic rulers and quite frequently in order to preserve their power, and sometimes to extend it, they were fighters too. The first among the chosen people to be publicly acclaimed by all was Saul, the son of Kish,[35] and after him came David who was not just an effective ruler but the founder of a dynasty as well.[36] His heirs, indeed, would rule for more or less four hundred years and only ceased when finally the Babylonians invaded and deported almost everybody even from Jerusalem itself.[37] There was, we know, a period of exile then and when a remnant did return they were no more than tolerated subjects of a foreign power. And yet the chosen people never ceased to hope and dream about a future messianic age when once again a son of David would emerge and sit upon their throne.

But let us for a moment go back to the earlier and royal years and in particular to David who, as we are told, was of the family of Jesse and had spent his youthful years providing for his father's sheep. Then God, who had his own plans, intervened and, as a later psalmist in the temple sang,

> took him away from the sheepfolds.
> From the care of the ewes he called him
> to be shepherd of Jacob his people,
> of Israel, his own possession.[38]

That was certainly a most important moment in the history of the chosen people and it was a moment which was well remembered too. Indeed it was quite frequently recalled and celebrated by the people, maybe even every year. And in the temple, in the presence of the reigning king, a soloist would sing:

> The Lord swore an oath to David;
> he will not go back on his word:
> 'A son, the fruit of your body
> will I set upon your throne.'[39]

Indeed, the people felt that, in some way, this family of David would continue on and on and would be always there.

> His dynasty shall last for ever[40]

they proclaimed. And they kept on proclaiming that belief, despite the fact that after the destruction of Jerusalem there was no longer any Jewish throne at all.

However let us focus just a little more on those years when there was a king residing in Jerusalem. He had, we know, a palace and let us presume that it was there that he was often to be found. But there were times when he would have been seen within the temple too. He would have been there for the celebration of the most important feasts including that one which gave thanks for his divine election and at which the psalm which speaks about the oath of God would have been solemnly declaimed. But there were other times as well when he would have decided to go there and one of them was surely when he knew that he would have to lead his army into battle and that it was necessary to receive a special blessing and the prayers of all. Indeed there is one psalm which seems to call to mind just such a situation. It begins with somebody, perhaps a priest, expressing in a prayer the wish that in this hour of need God would support and help the king and grant him his request.

> May the Lord answer in time of trial;
> may the name of Jacob's God protect you,[41]

30

he intones. And then, when all the people have contributed their own few lines of prayer (verse six appears to be a congregational refrain), a single voice, perhaps that of a prophet, solemnly proclaims:

> I am sure now that the Lord
> will give victory
> to his anointed.[42]

I do not know how often such a statement proved itself to be true prophesy but I do know that the Jewish people kept on using this same psalm long after the destruction of Jerusalem and the removal of their king. It was as if they felt that somehow God, through somebody, would one day overcome all evil in their lives and give them once again the freedom they desired.

There was, apart from military ones, another reason why the king was given special mention in the temple psalms. It was so that throughout his reign, and with the grace of God, he might rule justly and thereby allow all those within his kingdom to both live and grow in peace.

> O God give your judgement to the king,
> to a king's son your justice,
> that he may judge your people with justice
> and your poor in right judgement,[43]

a psalmist in the temple prayed. But, if he did, it should be noted that the psalmist was concerned not just for all the subjects of the king but in a special way for those who are, in every age, most frequently neglected and ignored.

> May he defend the poor of the people
> and save the children of the needy,[44]

he continued and we like to think that, when he heard those words, the king would have been moved to some extent at least to do as was desired. It is, perhaps, worth noting that the king himself is not described as praying in the psalms, that was the function of the people as a whole and of the temple priest. But it should certainly be noted that in post-exilic days this psalm would have in some way kept alive the hope that one day in the future there would be a messianic king who would fulfil the expectations of the people and reveal God's goodness and his justice in a very special way.

There was, as I have said, no king in those last Jewish centuries for other nations ruled the Middle East: the Persians and the Greeks and then finally the Romans. But, in any case, our brief reflection here upon the royal power should lead us not to some succeeding earthly power, such as the Jews may have expected or as we possess today. It should lead us instead to that 'king-personality' which is in all of us and which, for our development, must grow. Of course to grow successfully that 'personality' will need a lot of help from others like the 'scholar' and the 'prophet' and the 'sage'. But with their help, and with the grace of God who is the King of kings, it should be able to direct and organise our lives in such a way that what is able to attack and to destroy us will be kept at bay and elements within ourselves which are essential to our own development, but which can be so easily ignored, will have the space and opportunity to grow. And then we will ourselves experience the way of inner satisfying peace.

LIFE

Introduction

We must move now from people who appear to us as we read through the psalms to something which is in them all. It is their varying reactions to the One who, as they come to realise, has made them for himself and who, moreover, is in fact continuously seeking them. And so we must reflect a little on the chosen people as they grope for God and on those moments too when they cannot do very much at all but wait. Furthermore we must reflect about the need which they discover in themselves to be converted, purified and changed and after that about the joy which they experience when God invades their lives and makes it possible for them to burst into a song of heartfelt praise. All of this, of course, has much to do with moods but in itself what we are touching here is something much deeper. We are entering that area, if I can use that word at all, that central, silent area within ourselves where God's own Spirit mingles with our own and then, if we allow it, brings us stage by stage into the fullness of that life for which we yearn and for which we are made.

Seeking

We seek. We seek the Lord? Of course! At least we seek fulfilment of ourselves and happiness. But happiness, if it is true, is in itself no more than our side of that same reality which on the other is the life of God himself. And so, in seeking happiness, we all would seem to be in fact desiring him. And so we all can say, or learn to say, those well-known and attractive words,

> O God, you are my God, for you I long,
> for you my soul is thirsting.[1]

They, as some will recognise, are the initial words of one particular psalm and one to which we will have reason later to return. But for the moment, as we say them in a prayerful way let us accept and quietly absorb the meaning they imply: that we ourselves have been created with a need for him whose life is infinite and so 'to seek him' is the most important thing that we can do.

And so we seek the Lord. It may take time to find him and we may at times discover that we have in fact been going down some other road which is, in fact, no more than just a cul-de-sac. The chosen people of the Bible frequently, as we are told, did that! Indeed, as soon as they escaped from Egypt and received the first instalment of the freedom they desired, they failed to recognise it as the gift it really was. And then, when they began to settle in a land which they could call their own, they were attracted to the comforts which they found and easily exchanged the worship of the God who had delivered them for other things which were but deified delights. And so we find the more prophetic elements among them standing up and saying that their new-found idols were no more than

silver and gold,
the work of human hands[2]

and that they should be careful, for their makers will come to be like them and so will all who trust in them.[3]

Some people paid no heed of course, but others did and reconsidered the direction of their lives and rediscovered in themselves their deeper and their purer needs and, guided by those prophets, turned around and sought again, and in a better way, the Lord who offers to us all the real and everlasting life.

And so they sought the Lord. They sought 'the face of God', to use a phrase which we discover in a number of the psalms. It is, as somebody once said to me, a fascinating phrase, but it is also one which seems to have the implication that God can, in fact, be actually seen. That was, perhaps, to some extent the case in Egypt where the phrase itself, as far as I can ascertain, originated, for it was apparently the custom there in pagan temples to unveil, from time to time, the statue of the deity associated with a particular temple. The Jews, however, as we know, did not have any statues to unveil. They were forbidden to have any by the very first commandment of their Law. God was, they knew, beyond all that the human eye could see and yet it does seem that they knew as well this pagan phrase and even kept it, as a kind of souvenir, and used it in connection with a temple situation too. Indeed, does not that psalmist, whom we have already met, declare to God,

I gaze on you in the sanctuary,[4]

and is there not another who, while very far away from that most sacred spot, desired with all his heart to be there once again?

When can I enter and see
the face of God?[5]

he longingly enquired. He knew that in the temple God, in some way, could in fact be 'seen'!

This second psalmist speaks, moreover, of his yearning for the temple and the Lord, who could be found there, as a 'thirst'. A 'thirst' which is, he says, like that of a mountain deer

that yearns for running streams.[6]

It was, perhaps, an image which occurred to him when he was in some quiet and secluded spot and looking at those graceful animals, so sensitive to any sign or whiff of danger, as they made their way with care and with determination to the life-restoring water they required. If only he, in his own way, could do the same! He knew, however, that his 'thirst' was leading him, not just to the Creator who could be admired in everything but to the One who had revealed a mighty love which only those who gathered in

the house of God[7]

were able to experience. And so he longed to reach the Holy Place itself.

But here, when thinking of the love which God has for us all, we touch upon the other side of our expectant search. It is that, while we seek the Lord, he is already seeking us. It is that, while we want to find the Lord, he wants much more to find each one of us. And that is something which, of course, is very well expressed by him who wrote the so-called 'Hound of Heaven' psalm.[8] But it is also something which is often indicated when a psalmist speaks about the Lord who 'looks' at us and 'gazes' on us, too.

> From the place where he dwells he gazes
> on all the dwellers on the earth,[9]

One of them declares. Indeed on some occasions we can hear another yearning for that gaze to penetrate into the very centre of his being and, in doing so, allow him to experience the healing and the happiness which he so much desires.

> Let your face shine on your servant[10]

is a good example. But what we can say is that it seems as if the psalmist here has come to realise the marvellous truth: that seeking God is, to a large extent, desiring and allowing him to seek and to discover us!

Waiting

I remember being at a seminar on prayer some years ago and many of the people there were speaking about 'seeking God' and how they went about it. Then, quite suddenly, an elderly participant who had been getting somewhat irritated intervened. 'It has to do with waiting too,' he growled and quoted, to support his claim, the opening lines of what I recognised to be a psalm.

> I waited, I waited for the Lord
> and he stooped down to me;
> he heard my cry.[11]

That stopped the conversation for a while! And yet, as everybody recognised his contribution was a valuable one, for up till then there had been something of a tendency to speak, and so to think, of prayer as if it were a DIY affair, which it of course is not. Prayer does require some effort on our part but in the last analysis it is, as I have intimated, the activity of God's own Spirit mingling with our own.[12] And so, in order to co-operate with that transforming Spirit we have frequently to learn the art of waiting, too!

For some, of course, there may appear at times to be no other option possible! They simply have to wait. I think especially of those who are unwell, of those who suffer from some sickness or disease, of those who have some crippling disability. And some of these may, like their many predecessors in the psalms, cry out for help to God.

O Lord, do not forsake me[13]

one of them, a sufferer whose body we are told is burning with a fever, cries. And others, after listing all their aches and pains as people who are sick are wont to do, ask God 'How long?' 'How long must we endure?' And yet, while they may not hear any answer nor feel any physical relief, the very fact that they appeal to God is in itself a sign for us that God is somehow with them still and that he is assisting them to seek the grace which can and will, in his own time, grow into wholeness and eternal happiness.

I think as well of those who, whether they are physically sick or not, are harassed and oppressed and who, although they may have done no wrong at all, know that they have in fact no legal rights and that there is not anything that they can do to change or to improve their lot. The world is full of them! They are the poor, the widows and the orphans, and 'the little ones' whom nobody protects.

O Lord … come to my rescue!
Save my life from these raging beasts,[14]

rails one of them who lived in Bible times. He knew that in the past God had revealed himself as one who had compassion on the outcast and the underdog and hoped, no doubt, with all his heart that somehow God would intervene again, this time for him. And in a way, for people such as him, God often does. He may not seem to change the unjust situation in which those who suffer live but he can often give, as many of the psalms which we have seen reveal, some helpful and prophetic word which can in turn help those who hear it to discover some degree of peace within themselves and so, with confidence renewed, to battle on.

But even when we are not sick or worried by society an element of waiting is essential in our prayer. Indeed those very people whom so many may consider to be experts in this field, such as contemplative religious, would most surely be the very first to say that this is true. They know, from long experience, that prayer is often staying still in mind as well as body while, at a much deeper level, we keep yearning and desiring and expecting God to come. One of the first to write about this quiet kind of prayer was possibly John Cassian[15] who had visited the early monks in Egypt and then promulgated what they told him in the west. But he said too that, if we want to cultivate this inner stillness, it would be an excellent idea to have a prayer-verse which we can repeat and he, then, even recommended one:

O God, come to our aid.
O Lord, make haste to help us.[16]

Saying such a verse, he taught, can help us to dispel the many and distracting thoughts which constantly invade our minds and, at the same time, help us to prepare ourselves to welcome him who can fulfil our deepest needs and who most certainly will come. It is, moreover, one which has been chosen by the Church as the official opening invocation for each section, or each Hour, of its own Daily Prayer.

But let me here conclude this 'waiting' chapter with two images, both taken from the psalms.

The first one is that of a watchman who is waiting for the dawn. We can, perhaps, imagine him beside a warming fire as he sits in a silent and contented way aware that all is at that moment well and that the day which will release him from his work has almost come. In such as him the temple worshippers perceived an image of themselves:

> Let the watchman count on daybreak
> and Israel on the Lord[17]

they sang. And here I am reminded of a Hindu saying which expresses this same kind of certain expectation in an even stronger way. It says that death is no more than the quenching of a candle for the light of day has dawned! But even now, as Scripture and our own experience can testify, there can in fact be many dawns, many comings of the Lord. They do, of course, not come as regularly as the rising of the sun, but when they do and when they find us ready they are able to refresh us in a way which few will say has not been worthwhile waiting for.

The second image is that of a servant and the mistress of the house. Let us imagine for a moment that the servant is a young girl who is sitting in the corner of a room. She may be doing something useful or she may be simply sitting there but she, in either case, is conscious, very conscious, of the presence of her mistress and she is prepared and ready to respond to any sign or indication which that lady of the house may give. We paint that picture in our minds and then perhaps we start to notice that that young girl sitting there attentively reflects what we, at times of quiet prayer, can sometimes be.

> Like the eyes of a servant
> on the hands of her mistress,
> so our eyes are on the Lord, our God.[18]

And so this calming psalmist helps us to appreciate the fact, which we perhaps already know, that 'being there', just 'waiting on the Lord', can often be enough! God is content, he seems to say, when we discover that the only thing to do for the moment is to be still and sensitive to his abiding presence though of course prepared to notice and to welcome any sign or indication of his will which he may subsequently give.

Repenting

> Have mercy on me, God, in your kindness.
> In your compassion blot out my offence.[19]

The psalmist whom we meet in this most famous of the penitential psalms is very conscious of his faults but he is even more aware of God's unending mercy. Mercy! Let me pause here for a while for 'mercy' is a word which can be easily misunderstood. It does not mean, as some may think, a substituted attitude in God who up until then may have been angry and annoyed with us. God cannot have a substituted attitude and much less one which would depend on what we do, like wanting to repent. He is himself unchangeable and so to speak about his 'mercy' must refer to something which is constant in himself, though now perhaps appreciated in another way. And therefore it must mean his 'love', his radiating and creative love, but understood as it was not before, that is as totally gratuitous and undeserved. Indeed this is suggested in the psalm itself, for 'mercy' is associated there with God's 'compassion' and a little later on with his own 'loving kindness' while it could be noted that the Hebrew word from which it comes suggests a mother's womb![20] And so, can we not say that in this psalm the psalmist feels as does a child who knows that it has misbehaved but, at the same time, knows that all will be forgiven for its mother's love is very great, indeed?

And yet the psalmist is very much aware of his own sinfulness. He does not tell us in what way he sinned but that he did there is for him no doubt.

> My offences truly I know them;
> my sin is always before me,[21]

he declares. And then he seems to see that, while he may have done what he should not have done or failed to do what he knew was required, the sin in him goes deeper still, deeper than his actions and omissions, deeper than his words and thoughts, deeper even than his individuality itself.

> O see, in guilt I was born,
> a sinner was I conceived,[22]

he cries, but not despairingly, for if his human nature (which of course is ours as well) is paralysed by some contagious virus God, he knows, can only see that as an opportunity to exercise his healing and all-powerful love. And so all will be well. That love, as every page of Scripture testifies, is greater than the soul-destroying power of even 'universal sin'!

And so he simply asks the Lord to take it all away!

> O purify me, then I shall be clean;
> O wash me, I shall be whiter than snow.[23]

Purify me! Wash me! Make me clean! I wonder if these metaphors, for metaphors of course they are, could have been taken from what must have been a regular event which in his early days the psalmist would have frequently observed. I am referring to the washing of his clothes, and those of all his family as well. If so, do we not have here once again, at least implied, a feminine and a maternal image of the God which many people sadly think of as forbidding and severe. And if we call him 'Father', as we have been taught to do, do not the whole of revelation and the verses of this penitential psalm point to the fact that his paternity transcends the limitations of its earthly kind and that the qualities which we admire so much in mothers are in him as well? They surely do. It is no wonder that the contrite and repentant psalmist feels that all will be, in God's own way, made well.

And yet there is another thing for which the psalmist asks. It is not only to be cleansed but to be totally renewed. He seems to know that without inner transformation any new beginning will likely end up as did the last! And so we find him asking God for some injection of 'new life' or, keeping to the biblical expression, for another and a better heart and for a spirit which is stronger than his own.

> A pure heart create for me, O God,
> put a steadfast spirit within me,[24]

he devoutly prays. And that, of course, is what the good and loving God, who is Creator of all things, desires to do. But what the psalmist may not have perceived to the extent that we are able to today, is that that Spirit which God gives to us is his and that the life which we receive is, therefore, both divine and altogether new.

Praising

Praise is fitting for loyal hearts,[25] the psalmist sings. And maybe we should add that it is necessary, too, for 'loyal hearts' are those who really know that God is good and people such as that can have a great desire to praise him and, indeed, to tell the world about the things which he has done. And that was certainly the case with many of the singers of the psalms. But even those who seem to spend a lot of time bewailing their misfortune were in fact, we could say, praising-people too. Indeed they frequently concluded lamentation-psalms with verses which are full of gratitude and even in the verses which lament they seem to recognise and to acknowledge that the Lord has all things in his care and that, despite the hardships which they have to undergo, he is himself both wise and very good! And there is praise in that! And so, as we take up the different psalms and use them for our prayer today we should perhaps learn from the Jews themselves who put them all into a single volume which they called the *Tehillim*, or Songs of Praise,[26] for that is how they all in some way seemed to them!

But one could ask perhaps 'how did those people know that God is good?' or 'how could they have been so sure?' And some of course, if they could answer us, would say that they were so convinced because they had experienced his goodness in their lives. And if we were to ask them 'how was that?', they would no doubt be ready to elaborate and say that God had saved them from some illness or disease or, maybe, from the machinations of some evil-doers who were living in their midst. But then some

others, if we asked them, would perhaps begin to speak about the
Exodus event because that was, they knew, the one great act of
God which had affected everyone and it, moreover, was the one
in which the people of their day could still in some strange way
participate.[27] And so we find it mentioned in the temple psalms
and sometimes even stage-by-stage as if each were itself a reason
for rejoicing and for praise.

> He divided the red sea in two …
> He made Israel pass through the midst …
> Through the desert his people he led …

A certain psalmist sang[28] of these acts of God and all the people
in the temple, knowing that they too were being guided day-by-
day on their own journey through this often problematic life, may
have responded to each line with what appears to be a
congregational refrain:

> for his love endures for ever.[29]

And if some of those individuals had their own special reasons,
too, for giving thanks and praise they may have felt that, while
they were important for themselves, they were as well the signs
they needed to assure them that they were in fact participating in
the Paschal Mystery which the story of the Exodus, in its own
way, revealed.

Those people who desired to give God thanks and praise may
have at times assembled in each other's homes. That seems to be
what is suggested by the 'poor man' who had been in some way
blessed by God and who, in gratitude, invited then his friends to
come and celebrate with him.

> Glorify the Lord with me.
> Together let us praise his name[30]

he called. But for the most part it was probably within the temple
of Jerusalem itself that all these grateful celebrations would have
taken place. And there this just-now-quoted psalm would have

most certainly at times been sung and in the presence of a larger fellowship than would have ever gathered in a house! And there a much more solemn liturgy of praise, which does not mean an unexciting one, would have been celebrated in the company of many, some of whom would have arrived as pilgrims from afar. And so the individual who wanted to give thanks and praise could find that he, or she, was part of a community much vaster than is generally felt!

Those people who had gathered in the temple to give God their heartfelt thanks and praise would first, no doubt, have spent a little while reflecting on some chosen readings which recalled for them the major things that God had done but then they would of course have broken into song. The psalms themselves are evidence of that. But they did more for, as we can discover in those very psalms, those people in the temple must have frequently accompanied their singing with the music of

> the ten-stringed lyre and the lute[31]
> with the murmuring sound of the harp[32]

and no doubt with a lot of other instruments as well. And that itself would have enhanced the quality of their thanksgiving celebration. But we can be fairly sure, I think, that with that song and music flowing through them all the time a few, at least, would have got up … and actually danced! Indeed does not the psalmist of the psalter's final psalm seem to address the total congregation and invite all those in front of him to come and do just that?

> Praise him with the sound of trumpet,
> praise him with lute and harp.
> Praise him with timbrel and dance,[33]

he calls. And maybe we remember too how it had been recorded that when all the people crossed the sea and realised that they were safe and actually free, they also sang and played their timbrels and, as Scripture says, they danced.[34] Was that perhaps the archetypal celebration of them all?

But there is even more that we can say. It is that every worshipper in every age is part, not only of a human choir, but of a cosmic orchestra as well. All things participate in one great universal symphony! At times the psalmist, like ourselves, seems to admire the different pieces, great and small. We see him, for example, gazing as it were with wonder at the flowing rivers, at the animals that roam and roar and at the trees and mountains and the seas. And then we hear him say to God:

All these things look to you.[35]

Another psalmist seems to feel, however, that, in some way, he himself has to call forth each part of nature if they all are to participate completely in this 'symphony of everything'!

Praise him, sun and moon,
praise him shining stars,[36]

he sings. But maybe that is no more than another way of saying that he is prepared and ready now to be the mouthpiece of all things which do not of themselves possess a conscious and a grateful voice![37] And that is surely what he is. As for the one who really calls forth each and every part of nature it is certainly no other than the Spirit of the Living God and so, we can say that in everything, including humankind itself, and through that humankind, God can be truly glorified![38]

LIVING SIGNS

Introduction

Having seen some of the many types of people who are hidden in the psalms and having thought about some of the most important ways in which they can be found relating to their God, we must now look at how that God revealed himself to them. He is, we know, in his own inner life invisible and so of course it had to be through ordinary and created things that he was able to give them a glimpse of who he really is. And so, to take an obvious example, through the shepherd caring for his flock he let them see that he was a concerned and caring God and through the king, whom we have seen already from a different point of view, he manifested something of his all-controlling and effective power. But there were other images as well. There was the image of the mother who embraces with undying love her often wayward child, there was the image of the stronghold and the shield which in the heat of battle offers shelter and protection and there were those images of water and of light which in their different ways suggest to all of us life, happiness and joy. All these we will consider here but let us do so so that we will come, not only to appreciate some of the images through which the psalmist found his God, but also to perceive more readily the ones through which God now reveals himself to us.

The Shepherd

I have a photograph which someone gave me many years ago. It shows two rather lengthy lines of sheep as they move across a plain in Galilee and at their head, where they converge, there can be seen the distant figure of the shepherd who is leading them. No doubt he knows the way! No doubt he is prepared to notice any sign of danger to his flock and no doubt, if some danger does arise, he will know how to cope with it so that the sheep which follow him can safely journey on! Such was indeed the shepherd's role in what we now call Bible-times. While my treasured photograph implies that one can see that type of shepherd still, for those who saw him then he was an image and a sign of God, the super-shepherd of us all.

The Jewish people had of course a very special reason for delighting in this image for they were themselves a people who had travelled on a journey and who had to learn to recognise the one who could protect and lead them as they made their way towards a hoped-for Promised Land. Moses was, we know, the leader whom they followed throughout all those struggling years but Aaron also played a shepherd's part and both indeed are mentioned in the plaintive psalm which a later psalmist sang.

> You guided your people like a flock
> by the hand of Moses and Aaron[1]

he declared, and hoped no doubt that God, through somebody, would do the same for him. But here as you can see he knew as well that, if those two outstanding leaders were the chosen people's special guides, God was himself the one who guided all. He was, according to another psalmist, the true shepherd who

> brought forth his people like sheep;
> (and) guided his flock in the desert.[2]

And as life unfolded that awareness (that it is the Lord himself who is our guiding and providing shepherd) grew.

Of course when their nomadic lifestyle in the desert ceased and when the people found themselves within the structures of a kingdom, the idea of God as shepherd must have given way, to some extent, to other and more telling ones. And yet because their past was with them still, as ours is still with us, they kept the thought of God as shepherd too and used it in their prayers, especially perhaps when they were conscious of an extra need for guidance or security. And so we find a psalmist praying to that 'super-shepherd' when he was oppressed by 'evil-doers', and indeed when those around him may have been so too.

Save your people;
Bless Israel your heritage.
Be their shepherd
and carry them for ever,[3]

he, with hope, exclaimed. And later when the kings of Israel, who were at times called shepherds too, were seen to have completely let the people down and were themselves in fact destroyed, the thought that God alone was their real shepherd consequently came more strongly into focus.[4] He it was who could not only lead them on but even carry them as well!

The psalm which sings most eloquently of this super-shepherd comes most probably from later post-exilic times when many problems had been undergone and many had been somehow solved. It is the one which we have briefly seen at the beginning of this book, the one in which the psalmist with a calm and certain confidence, says that the Lord himself is his own shepherd now and that at last he has discovered that, to quote him:

there is nothing I shall want.[5]

He talks, we know, about new pastures too, those which are fresh and green[6] and seems to think at times about a life where, by the shepherd's crook and staff, he will be well-protected from all harm and absolutely safe. Perhaps because the author of the book of Revelation quotes some verses from this psalm when he is speaking about those who are already in white garments[7] and because we tend to use this psalm at funerals today we let it conjure up for us, too readily perhaps, a picture of the world to come. But, while that future life of happiness is certainly implied in this most favourite of psalms, let us not lose sight of the fact that its main message really is that God is with us here and now. It is that he is guiding us

along the right path[8]

every day – and that, just as the shepherd feeds those sheep which are not strong, he does the same for each of us, weak mortals that we are; although within the psalm this final thought is symbolised, not by the shepherd metaphor itself but by an added temple one: that of the banquet and the overflowing cup.[9]

The King
In a previous chapter we had reason to reflect upon the king but as a person who resided in Jerusalem and was a well-known figure there. We now must think about him, even see him, as a sign of God's own powerful presence in the world. And in particular, of course, we need to see how that awareness is reflected in the psalms.

And so let us imagine for a moment that we are among the people in the temple for the celebration of a most important feast. And let us, in imagination, look around and see the people and the choirs and, in the places which have been reserved for them and in their splendid robes, the consecrated priests. And then let us imagine that the moment for which everyone is waiting comes: it is that of the solemn entry of the king! He walks, with stately reverence, up to the sanctuary itself, and there he turns around and sits upon the throne which is prepared for him a little to the right of what the people know is, in a very special way, the place from which the Lord himself invisibly presides. And then a soloist, perhaps a temple prophet, starts to sing the famous words which, as we have them, are translated now:

The Lord's revelation to my Master:
'Sit on my right.'[10]

And all the people know that he, whom they can see, is the official representative of God's own majesty on earth!

The true king therefore is the Lord himself! The chosen people knew that well and even in the early days when they were choosing Saul. The prophet Samuel made sure of that![11] But later, when they no longer had any earthly king to rule them, circumstances led those who survived the Exile to become more conscious of the only sovereign who could give them a sense of who they really were.

The Lord is king![12]

they would exclaim,

The Lord is king, with majesty enrobed![13]

And in the temple all the people who had come together would bow low, and with the deepest reverence, before the beneficial but almighty power of God.

We are not sure in what way God revealed himself to those who gathered in the temple on those special post-exilic festive days. The experts say that it might have been through some special sacred ritual and they may well be right. In any case what seems quite certain is that, whatever ritual there may have been, it would have been interpreted and understood with the awareness of what oriental kings were like. Moreover, memories of powerful forces in creation and especially of those which took place when the covenant was made at Sinai, would have coloured their appreciation of the One whom they revered.[14] And so in what are definitely 'royal psalms' we still can hear the echo of those worshippers who could describe the garments of their transcendental king as

cloud and darkness[15]

and who could declare that his majestic power was like the fire and lightning of a thunder storm, or similar to some suchlike phenomenon.

A fire prepares his path; …
His lightnings light up the world, …
The mountains melt like wax
before the Lord and all the earth.[16]

Today, however, we do not have much experience of royal power and even less of that power which an oriental monarch would have had. But maybe most of us are able to recall some moments when we were held speechless by the power which flows through nature: in the sky or in the sea or by the awesome and breathtaking majesty which certain places can at times reveal. Such moments can, in their own way, help us when we take up and read today those so-called 'royal psalms'.

And yet while all the people then bowed low before the majesty of God they did so, not with reverential fear alone, but also with a spirit of thanksgiving and of joy. They knew that God, their mighty king, was wonderful and good and that he had done many things for them and that he could and would do much more. And so they sang as well as bowed, and many played their harps and other instruments and all helped one another to rejoice.

Shout to the Lord,[17]

they called.

With trumpets and the sound of the horn
acclaim the King, the Lord.[18]

He was, they knew, their one and only king and they were sure that he, who had delivered them from Egypt and from Exile too, would somehow overcome their present problems and bring them, and many others with them, into one great perfect kingdom which he would himself someday establish in their midst.

For he comes,
he comes to rule the earth,[19]

they sang and we can hear in that the early expectations of what we might today call the joy of an Advent certitude.

The Mother
The motherhood of God is quite a fascinating thought and one which many people like to talk and write about today. But if they do it is no merely modern idea but one which, for example, in the Middle Ages was quite popular and which among the Jews in Bible times was also on occasions found. Indeed we have already

seen, and to a small degree discussed, the psalm which talks about the mistress of the house on whom the servant keeps her eye and we have noted too that in the Hebrew language 'mercy' is a word which is related to the one which means a 'womb'. And so in this short section let us look at one more Scripture text: it is the psalm in which the psalmist says that he is like a child relaxing in his mother's arms and happy to be there. It is the psalm which represents, more strongly than we generally find, the biblical tradition that the Lord of everybody is a Mother for us too.

> A weaned child on its mother's breast,
> even so is my soul.[20]

It is unlikely that the psalmist could remember when he was himself just such a child but as he looked around him he could hardly not have noticed many children who were feeding at their mother's breast or resting in their arms. And as he looked he must have thought that their position viz-a-viz their mothers was quite comparable to his own relationship with God. Perhaps, however, it had not been always quite so close! Perhaps when he said that he was not proud or haughty he was thinking of a time when, looking back, it seemed that he had been so very busy doing many things, and trying even the impossible, and all the time without a real reliance on the God from whom, as he now knows, all blessings actually come. Perhaps! In any case he now has found the peace and the enfolding love which he has always, in his heart of hearts, desired.

That God is 'mother', and not just a 'father' and much less the rather terrifying deity which many people think, is something which indeed deserves to be proclaimed. The psalmist, I am glad to say, thought so as well. At least the last two lines of this short psalm appear to be an invitation to the whole community to come and to discover for themselves the tender love and the refreshment which that mothering divinity alone can give.

> O Israel, hope in the Lord
> both now and for ever,[21]

sings the singer of this psalm. But whether those few words were written by the psalmist who composed the lines which went before or whether they were added by some later editor to make a very personal confession suitable for temple use is something which we do not really know and which in fact need not concern us here. What is important is that these two final lines suggest that all who hear them can discover, if they try, that God is really like that mother who cannot forget, much less reject, her trusting and dependent child.[22] Indeed, as one much later writer says, 'true motherhood' is to be found in God;[23] all others, marvellous though they may be, are in the last analysis, but human and consoling signs although, of course, as signs they can lead us into that love which has no breaking point at all!

The Stronghold

There is a special group of images which reappear from time to time within the psalms and which we must refer to now. They are of military origin and, while the image of the 'stronghold' certainly is one of them, those of the 'refuge' and the 'shield' must be included too. And so must 'rock', although this last has implications which the others do not have.[24]

It is, of course, not difficult to understand how images like these, all taken from the world of warfare, should have crept so easily into the prayers of ordinary people to be used in ordinary times. For centuries, the Hebrew people had been fighting with the tribes and nations which did everything they could to oust them from the land where they desired to dwell, to say nothing of the civil wars such as the one between king Saul and David who was destined to succeed him. In each one of these there must have been occasions, indeed many, when the weary soldiers searched for some great rock behind which they could shelter or for the protection of a place where they could rest. And so in later times when individuals, who were not fighters in the field, felt that they were themselves in some way harassed or oppressed they took those very images and used them to describe the God in whom they now were putting all their trust.

My God is the rock where I take refuge;
my shield, my mighty hope, my stronghold,[25]

they would trustingly proclaim. And in the strong protective presence of that God, who was – they knew – invincible, they learned how to relax!

The 'stronghold' and the 'refuge' and the 'rock' par excellence of course was Zion or Jerusalem itself. To it the armies of successive enemies might and did come but, not until the Babylonians demolished it could any manage to break through its sturdy and encircling walls. It was, according to Isaiah, God's own special city and as long as he was there no foe would ever really enter it or hurt those whom it held! Indeed in such a situation it could be the enemy who was in fact at greater risk! And here I cannot help recalling that most strange occurrence which is mentioned in the second book of kings: that when the chosen people in Jerusalem awoke and rose one day they saw the army which till then had been besieging them completely vanquished and destroyed! Perhaps of course it was the work of some in-transit army but the Scriptures simply say 'it was the intervention of an angel of the Lord'.[26] And so we find that, as the meaning of that kind of story seeped into the minds and souls of those who would in later years assemble in the temple, they would say, and for the benefit of everybody, whether worried by invading armies or just by the ordinary problems of each day:

Your eyes have only to look
to see how the wicked are repaid,
you who have said 'Lord, my refuge!'
and have made the Most High your dwelling.[27]

The 'stronghold' which the people really needed was, of course, not that which is assured by city walls but that which is the strong enfolding presence of the Lord himself. That makes us think again, perhaps, of the preceding image of the loving mother who is the security and haven which her small and infant child requires, for images do tend to overlap! But the awareness that it is indeed the Lord himself who guards us and protects us came, as we might have expected, when there were no longer any 'walls' at all! It was when those who had returned from Exile to their ancient home found only ruins and, requiring all the consolation and encouragement which prophets of their day could give, rejoiced when one of them said that the Lord himself would be to them 'a wall, a wall of fire'.[28] The message was that even if they felt exposed to problems from all sides, they could in fact relax and know that they were well protected and quite safe![29] And once again, when we identify with them, we are perhaps reminded of the Spirit which envelops us and which, if it does not obliterate all that is able to annoy or worry us, can certainly keep all of them sufficiently at bay!

Water

Water is a fascinating, mesmerising thing! One can, as we all know, sit gazing at it for long periods, especially perhaps in summer-time, and come away refreshed. But water, while it often has this calming and restorative effect is in itself much more. It is, it could be said, the giver of all life. Indeed there are so many nations of the world today who know this only 'much too well' as they wait for the hoped-for and essential rains! The Jewish people knew it too and we are told that when Elijah had beseeched the Lord to end a long and soil-destroying drought he looked and gazed towards the sea until the cloud, which he on this occasion knew would come, appeared. And then, the rain began – and new life was made possible![30]

Indeed each year it was the rains which made the crops to grow and harvests to be plentiful. And then when all would have been gathered in, the people would rejoice and come together, too, to give God thanks for, as they knew, it is from him that growth and harvest ultimately come. It was, no doubt, on just such an occasion that a psalmist in the temple added to the general rejoicing his own words of gratitude and praise.

> You care for the earth, give it water,
> you fill it with riches.
> Your river in heaven brims over
> to provide its grain.[31]

But now of course there would have been not only grain and other products of the soil but healthy deer, as we have noticed earlier, and animals both great and small which could be used for eating and for sacrifice and, though it may not seem at first to have a profitable use, the pleasant singing of

the birds of heaven;
from the branches they sing
their song.[32]

Thanks to the rains there is each year a kind of paradise regained! What may or could have been a desert comes alive and often does so in an almost messianic way!

But humans, if they are to grow, need water too! There was indeed, within Jerusalem itself, a little stream called Siloam which guaranteed a good supply to all the dwellers there. It was invaluable, and especially when hostile armies came and stayed outside the city walls preventing the inhabitants from going out. And that in fact is what occurred when the Assyrians arrived and consequently caused much panic and despair. Indeed at such a moment that small stream within became the most important thing the people had! Isaiah, who was with them even said that, though it seemed to flow so gently, it was greater than those huge and powerful rivers, the Euphrates and the Tigris, which of course for him were symbols of the proud and overflowing empire of Assyria itself. The humble mini-river in Jerusalem was the reliable God-given one![33]

The waters of a river
give joy to God's city,[34]

a much later psalmist, influenced by this Isaian thought, proclaimed. And as he did, he too seemed to suggest that in his mind this mini-river, this so-gently flowing stream, meant more to him than merely flowing water. It was something almost mystical!

Water is in fact a sign of God himself. But here we should, I think, recall again those summer days when we may have been sitting silently beside a flowing stream and gently taking in the peace which it helped to make possible. They were the times when, looking back, we seemed to rise above the binding chain of nature, of which we are certainly a part, and when we saw intuitively that the water which was there in front of us was but an image of another kind which we in fact were drinking even then. It was perhaps the water which a wise man in the Bible called the gift of wisdom, wisdom which comes from above, wisdom which all people are invited to receive![35] But, if that is to some extent an adequate description, it is once again a psalmist who can help us to appreciate what that gift really is.

They drink from the stream
of your delight,[36]

he sings and those who truly seek the Lord and know how to sit still in his refreshing presence find, as did that psalmist, that he is indeed the very source of all that we call life!

Light
The Hebrew people saw one, we are told! It was when they were in the desert and it seemed to be, the author of the book of Exodus informs us, like a pillar made of fire. And as those people travelled on it went, it seemed, ahead of them and lighted up the way.[37] It was a sign, a sign that God himself was guiding them as they kept searching for a hoped-for promised land. And so in later centuries, when the descendants of those very people sang:

the Lord
(he) is my light,[38]

it would have been with thoughts like these in mind but with the extra knowledge that, although no longer in the desert, they themselves were on a kind of journey, too.

For many people it was through the words of prophets and of sages that the light they needed was obtained. And then of course there were the Scriptures which contained the treasured words of both and which were pondered carefully by 'scholars', as we saw. They too provided 'light'. I could quote in support of this some lines which those psalm-writing scholars wrote, but I have quoted the most quotable of them before. And so, let me just mention the petition of the psalmist who desired to find his way.

Send forth your light[39]

he prayed. He knew that in whatever way it came, through reading Scripture or through someone whom he met, it would lead him towards Jerusalem and to the temple where the Lord was waiting for him in a very special way.

The light which comes with every word of God, however, may in fact not come when we are actually listening to that word, or even when we are alone and reading it in private, but perhaps much later on when we are doing something else and in some other place. We can, indeed, be somewhat like a camera which points in one direction but, because the button marked 'delayed' has been pressed, does not go off at once but waits until a later time. But then, when we are ready and prepared, the word which we have pondered will light up our mind, and we will know what it is saying and rejoice.

In the morning
fill us with your love,[40]

a psalmist prayed and, while the 'word' is not explicitly referred to here, this is a verse which seems to say that what God wants to tell us will be understood when what we here might call the 'night' has passed!

And so the 'dawn', that start of yet another day, is the symbolic moment which anticipates the start of perfect and of everlasting life. It is a time, moreover, when religious people everywhere can find that they are drawn to some kind of expectant prayer and that, we know, was frequently the case among the Jews as well.

I will awake the dawn,[41]

one of them cried and down the ages others, who looked forward
to the joy which is to come, discovered too the value of that first-
light sacred hour. But if they did the 'dawn', just as a thought,
was often one which did not only promise what was still to come
but reinforced that promise with the memories of blessings past.
And so it must have been for those who could recall that morning
when, on looking out, the people saw that all who up until then
had been besieging them had simply disappeared![42]

Joy comes with dawn![43]

they could have said, remembering that time. But if they did they
would have only had one reason more to yearn with confidence
for yet another day, a day indeed which would not only overcome
the tears and sorrows of the 'night', but which would grow and
last for evermore!

Some people say that it was only in the second or third century
before the coming of our Lord that Jews began to focus with
conviction on a world which is to come. And that may well be
true.[44] And yet it is becoming more acceptable to say that, maybe,
certain rays of that still-future light already touched some of the
people who composed some of the early psalms.[45] Indeed there
are a number of attractive verses which suggest to us that life that
is to come. The final couplet of the shepherd psalm (psalm 22/23)
is one and others we will have a chance to look at and examine
in the chapter after this. So, for the moment, let me quote just one
verse which, with very certain hope, turns our attention to that
life of perfect happinesss and joy.

I am sure
I shall see the Lord's goodness
in the land of the Living.[46]

'Light' is not referred to here. This verse does not explicitly speak
of the 'dawn' but does it imply, and even helps us to desire, the
everlasting and all-satisfying day?

TRINITY

Introduction

We spoke in chapter one about the personalities whom we discover in the psalms and then about the moods and attitudes they had and, finally, about the God who had revealed himself to them. And then, in the three chapters following, we took each one of these in turn and, spoke of them again but this time in a more developed way. And now what we must do is take all these three elements again and try to see them in the context of the Trinity itself. But here because the factor which will be completely new is Christ, that all-inclusive personality and second person of the Trinity, we shall begin with him. And then we will reflect a little on the way the Holy Spirit moulds all those who use the psalter into Christ. And finally a word, if that is not too much, about the God from whom that Spirit comes - and to whom it, through that same Christ, returns!

Christ

Christ, for Christians, is of course at the very centre of their faith. He had, the first disciples knew, been one like them in every way although, as they began to add, 'but sin'.[1] But now they knew as well that he had been raised up by God[2] into a new and everlasting life. And so, as years went by, a number of the early Christians said that he had been enthroned as King of kings and others that he had become their Mediator and High Priest. And down through the ages both of those two thoughts remained and influenced, apart from other things, the Christian understanding of the psalms and our appreciation of the greater context in which they can now be prayed.

But first, before reflecting on the way that those two roles of Christ affect our praying of the psalms, let us say something of his earthly life for that can help us too. And so because we have already spoken of such people as the 'pilgrim', and the 'prophet' and the 'scholar' and the 'sage' let us say here that Jesus in his earthly life was all of these as well. He was a 'pilgrim' who not only set his face towards Jerusalem[3] but who, as leader of a new and greater Exodus, left everything behind and went to his eternal Father where he now prepares a place for all who follow him.[4] And we could also say that he, who would be later spoken of as one who had fulfilled the Scriptures, found in them the wonderful yet often piercing words which helped him at the time to understand his life on earth and which showed him, as well, the way he had to go.[5] And could we not say too that he was also something of a sage, this man of parables, who could, from the experience of life around, draw images to illustrate the message which he so desired to give? We surely could. But if the people of his time considered him to be in any category, it was certainly in that of prophet for he was a person who could make them see not only something of their own true selves but something of the God who made them, too.[6] And so throughout his earthly life while he recited many of the psalms, as he most surely did, he could have easily identified with many of the personalities which are, as we have seen, in them. And consequently as we use these psalms today, we can pick up in many of their lines the echo of his voice as well and so learn to identify, not only with a lot of people of the past, whose names of course we do not know, but with the one whose name is known to everybody and who is, of course, for us the perfect representative of all.

But then there is the good news of his resurrection, too! And that has given to a number of the psalms, or to a number of the verses in the psalms, a new and, for the prayerful reader, an exciting sense. To take but one example: on the feast of Pentecost itself St Peter, we are told, stood up and, as he preached to many who had gathered in Jerusalem, referred to one verse which, as Jews, they would most certainly have recognised. It was the verse which reads:

You will not leave my soul among the dead,
nor let your beloved know decay.[7]

Perhaps the psalmist, who had long before composed the psalm to which this verse belongs, was one of those who did glimpse something of the life which lies beyond the grave. Perhaps! But it was only with the coming of the Spirit that the meaning of this special verse within the context of the Paschal Mystery (that is within the mystery of Christ's own death and resurrection) became clear, and to this day it is associated with it still.[8]

St Paul was also one of those who preached the message of the resurrection. And, at least according to St Luke, he too supported what he said with verses taken from the psalms. Indeed he quoted that verse which has just been mentioned but he quoted too the one in which the Father seems to say,

You are my son.
It is I who have begotten you this day.[9]

It is a verse which may have originally been a prophetic statement made when some new king had been exalted and enthroned. It is a verse which later, when there was no longer any king upon the throne at all, suggested to the Jews a messianic monarch who would in the future give to everyone the freedom and the peace which they desired. But now, and ever since the first few years of Christianity, it has become a verse which speaks of Christ himself, of him who is the very special Son of God and who has been raised up and given for the benefit of all a new and royal and, indeed, a universal power.[10]

Sit on my right.[11]

God seems to say. And here we must bring back again that psalm which in the previous chapter we have seen. But now let us not stay with this enthronement verse, important though it is, but move on to another which refers to the selection of the perfect and eternal priest.

The Lord has sworn an oath
he will not change:

'You are a priest for ever,
a priest like Melchisedech of old.'[12]

Melchisedech, it should be said, is mentioned only briefly in
the Bible[13] but, because he offers sacrifice and since there is no
mention of his parents or of any children that he may have had,
he is a symbol for the author of the letter to the Hebrews of the
perfect and the everlasting priest.[14] But then of course for him,
who quotes this psalm, that perfect everlasting priest is Christ
himself, the one who intercedes for us,[15] the one through whom
we now are able to approach the Father of us all.

A story tells us how, about the year 1,100, a cleric from the
north of Ireland made his way down to the south and found
accommodation in a hostel in or not too far from Cork. He said
his prayers and then, as he discovered that the people of the place
were rude and noisy, felt that he should do all that he could to
help them to improve. And so, the story goes, he 'took his book-
satchel, brought out a psalter and began to preach'.[16] How
interesting! Presumably he knew his psalter fairly well and
probably he was familiar with the way that preachers of the time
picked out those verses from the psalms which could corroborate
their message of Good News. But that this cleric should have
preached with just the psalter as his guide and that he should
have presupposed, as I suppose he did, that such a method would
have been acceptable to people in a noisy hostel, must most surely
make us think!

Of course, as we have seen already, Paul and Peter seem to
have done much the same, although the closest that they got to
hostels may have been a prison here and there! But here, let us
look at another element of early Christian preaching and at how
it influenced the understanding of the psalms. It is the fact that
Jesus was condemned to death and crucified as if he were a
common criminal. It is a fact which the evangelists of course
narrated at some length but if they did it always was with help
from certain verses of the psalms. And so when they referred to
those who crucified him we can find the lines:

they divide my clothing among them.
They cast lots for my robe.[17]

And when they speak about the mocking and unruly crowd they use expressions which remind us of another verse in that same psalm:

> They curl their lips,
> they toss their heads.
> 'He trusted in the Lord,
> let him save him;
> Let him release him
> if this is his friend.'[18]

And then, of course, when Jesus is about to die, those words which now are so well-known are used:

> My God, my God,
> why do you forsake me?[19]

The telling of the Passion is, in fact, so interwoven with expressions taken from this psalm that it not only brings this psalm (and others too) into the very centre of the Paschal Mystery, but must have given to all those who heard that Passion preaching first the means for understanding and accepting what was, in itself, an unacceptable event. And that not least because the psalmist in this case was able to conclude his song with verses full of gratitude and praise!

And so we can say that the psalms speak of the total mystery, the resurrection and the death, or that they do so fairly clearly to all those who have received the gift of Christian faith.[20] Indeed, one early Christian writer wrote:

> In the psalms we see not only Jesus being born, but we further see him facing his bodily passion for our salvation, resting in the tomb, rising from it, ascending into heaven sitting at the right hand of the Father.[21]

There is, I know, one problem here for 'being born' does not appear to be a part of the essential Paschal Mystery and so some comment on it seems to be required. Moreover, that one psalm-verse which is often used to illustrate the Bethlehem event, the one in which the Father seems to say:

It is I who have begotten you this day,[22]

is not in the New Testament, as we have seen, or a Christmas verse at all. And yet, although this verse is still used on the feast of the Nativity, the Liturgy itself, we must admit, looks forward in the very celebration of that feast to what will be commemorated when the Easter celebration comes. And so we can and must say that, while psalms can slide and be applied to other, even many other, things, their secondary meanings must be always rooted in, and draw their inspiration from, their Paschal one if their true Christian value is to be perceived.

A psalm, however, which did not get much attention in the very early preaching of the Church, except for one verse which need not concern us here, is one which Jesus would in fact have sung when celebrating the Last Supper meal.[23] It is one of the Hallel Psalms[24] and, while as such it would have been used by the Jews to celebrate the Exodus event, the Christians who accepted it into their Liturgy used it to illustrate that greater Exodus which Jesus on that night of nights anticipated in a sacramental way. It is a psalm which shows some signs of having been a song used as the pilgrims to Jerusalem arrived before the 'gates of holiness'[25] but now the more important verses surely are the ones which mention death but then go on to celebrate what seems to be so clearly both a new and resurrected life.

I was thrust down,
thrust down and falling[26]

the reflecting psalmist sang, but then he quickly adds:

The Lord's right hand has triumphed;
his right hand raised me![27]

And again we find a psalm which teaching clerics, whether of the celtic kind or not, could easily have used to help and to encourage those who listened, not just to appreciate the mystery of Christ, but actually to become a part of it as well. Indeed, this psalm has echoed down the centuries and has become for those who use the Prayer Book of the Church the Sunday psalm par excellence; it marks our weekly Easter day, the day around which Christian life has for so long revolved.

Our celtic cleric preached the Good News with the psalter in his hand! He could have used those special verses which already had been singled out by preachers as the Christ-revealing ones and which we have, though briefly, looked at here.[28] But he could have used almost any of the other psalms as well for all in some way, as the Christian Church began to see more clearly every day, reflected by anticipation him who would personify them all. The lamentations, for example, as the use of some by the evangelists suggests, anticipate for us the passion-prayer of Christ himself and every psalm of gratitude and praise which we take up reflects, to some extent, the joy of his own resurrection-life. And so we could say that the psalter as a whole is the Good News itself, although of course proclaimed not with the cold precision of dogmatic logic but in prayer and in community-involving song.

****

The psalms, indeed, are primarily prayers. The celtic cleric whom we met knew that as well. In fact the story tells us that when he arrived at that monastic hostel, where he was to stay, he took his psalter and not only read the psalms, or part of them, to others but used them for his own prayer as well.[29] And in the very early Church the Christians, and especially the ones who came from Jewish backgrounds, must have often done the same. St Luke in fact suggests that even when he was in chains, as he so often was, St Paul not only prayed but sang the psalms,[30] while in Jerusalem St James wrote in the letter which we still possess:

If anyone is happy
let him sing a psalm[31]

But let us come back to the celtic world for there we find an ancient poem which purports to be the grateful exclamation of a prayerful priest who has discovered, after many years, the long-lost psalter of his youth! He says how glad he is to have it once again and then towards the end declares:

> You are a token and a sign
> to men of what all men must heed.
> Each day your lovers learn anew
> God's praise is all the skill they need.[32]

God's praise! The psalms, indeed, express it and they teach all those who use them to express it, too!

The psalms lead us into an atmosphere of prayer. They do because they are themselves the prayers of many people and because they have been moulded by their constant use within the temple in Jerusalem. They lead us into prayer because they have been understood as prayers which speak, in different ways, of Christ himself. Some seem, indeed, as we have seen to be the very words which he himself once used and others seem, as we have also seen, to be addressed to him, or maybe linked to him in some particular way. And so it was a custom in the early and the medieval Church to give to every psalm a Christian title so that they could more easily be prayed with Christ himself in mind. And so some psalms were said to be the voice of Christ to the Father, and others were accepted as the voice of Christ (perhaps with a prophetic accent) to the Church, while others still were understood to be the voice of the apostles (preaching Christ).

In fact, it may be interesting to note, that, of the many lists of Christian titles, that one which enjoyed perhaps the greatest circulation was the one composed by St Columba of Iona[33] and it is from his that I have quoted here.

But, while such titles can be of considerable help and while they do acknowledge the diversity within the psalms there is perhaps a need within ourselves to simplify procedures and to find some kind of all-including formula which we can also use. And, fortunately, St Augustine thought so too! In his classic commentary on the psalms he wrote:

There can hardly be found any words in the psalms which are not the words of Christ and his Church, whether of Christ alone or of the Church alone.[34]

And then, adapting Pauline teaching, he says in another place that Christ, who is the head, and his body which is growing still, and which we call the Church, form but a single person.[35]

So, within the psalms, it is the total Christ who prays and who in prayer receives the gift of God which is the Holy Spirit. And our contribution, whether it be one of asking or receiving, of lamenting or of praising or, indeed, of musing quietly, is therefore part of the activity in us of Christ and of his Holy Spirit and has, therefore, both the value and the dignity of being so.

One of the great advantages which this awareness has is that it helps us to accept as prayer those verses which we feel that Christ could not have said. Some verses do have words which he would not have used but we can still consider them as part of Christ's own prayer, although of course not said by him who is the head, but by the not-yet-perfect members of his body which is growing still. They verbalise the anger which all those who yearn can find within themselves when they find that they cannot have what they desire or need. They are in fact the outbursts of a moment, though, if we are honest, we will be prepared to say that such an outburst can, of course, take place in our own lives as well. But, fortunately, if we take the psalter as a whole, and that is something which we ought to do, those cursing-verses are not only balanced but outweighed by all the other much more Christ-like lines which we prefer to say and into which we can most surely grow.

The second reason why this Augustinian approach can be of help when we are meditating on the psalms is that it keeps us conscious all the time that there are many others in this body which is Christ. And so when we take up a psalm and read it and discover that it does not at that very moment correspond to how we feel, we can at least accept the fact that there could be a lot of others in the world to whom it does apply and who, in Christ, are actually part of us. For them, perhaps, we have been called that very day to pray and they, in some way, may depend on us to do so just as we depend on others to do much the same for us. Indeed, awareness of the total Christ can make us conscious that we are not only called to pray for others but to pray with them as well. I can remember one young lady telling me that, while she liked to take the Prayer Book of the Church each day, what sometimes kept her going was the thought that there were others in the world who maybe at that very moment were about to do the same and that, in some strange way, they were indeed with her, and she with them, as she prayed by herself those ancient prayers. And so, as each one tries to enter into what the psalms suggest, the Body as a whole may find the spiritual energy it needs and it can consequently grow!

Spirit

The Spirit prays in us. Of course we pray as well. We say our words and, when we use the psalms, we say the ancient hallowed words which have been lovingly passed down. But, if we do, it is not just because we want to, though that is important too, but more because another Spirit is controlling ours and bringing us, through those same words, to him from whom it comes. That Spirit comes from God and is, indeed, at work in us when we begin to pray.

But that Spirit may have first to still our often very restless souls. It has, quite frequently, to come and hover over us and bring the 'tohubohu' of our minds, to use a Genesis expression,[36] into a receptive calm. And this, according to St Basil, the great, Cappadocian monk and Bishop, is what happens in a specially effective way when we take up the psalter and begin to pray a psalm.

> The psalm brings tranquillity to souls. It controls wild and turbulent thoughts,[37]

he wrote. And so, before we even start a psalm and certainly when we are reading it, we need to let that Spirit come and lead us through the psalm-words until we become, according to that same part of the Book of Genesis, the image and the likeness of the One from whom the Spirit, and the Word itself, has come.[38]

But this great, all-pervading Spirit which comes from above is able to unite us too with all those others who are ready to receive it, too. Of course, when it does that it makes us all a part of that delightful fellowship which by a psalmist was so highly praised!

How good and pleasant it is, when brothers dwell in unity,[39]

he exclaimed, though here we certainly must be prepared to read these words, not only as they are, but as they would be with a non-exclusive terminology as well! But, for the moment, let us come back to St Basil for he, who was responsible for a monastic settlement, was very conscious of the need for good and loving inter-personal relationships and also of how much the singing of the psalms together can facilitate their growth. It can, he said, dispel or overcome the many things which, on another and more superficial level, keep us separate and apart. And at the same time it can bring us all into an atmosphere of harmony and peace!

For how could you regard as an enemy one with whom you raise up a single voice to God?[40]

he asked. Indeed St Hildegarde, that medieval mystic and superior of quite a large religious house who is today collecting many fans, wrote to her Bishop and, despite the fact that he had wanted her community to simply 'say the psalms', said that 'to sing them' was important too. The singing and the music, she insisted, can

transform and shape the performance of our inner being towards praises of the Creator.[41]

She did not say that this 'transforming' can enable that 'one voice', of which St Basil spoke, to come more quickly into being. But, since that is what occurs, she will, I hope, not mind if I restate it now. And I will add that that 'one voice', which comes from our 'transforming' and from our uniting with each other through the psalm-words which we sing, is that of no one less than Christ, the Christ who is the perfect image of the Father and who can include us all!

Indeed the Spirit working in us opens up our hearts, not just to those who sing with us, but to a lot of others too and even to those very people who upset and worry us the most. Such may have been the case when one particular psalmist, in whose psalm there are more cursing-verses than there are in any other, took his pen and wrote:

in return for my love they accuse me while I pray for them.[42]

Much later, in our present century in fact, the well-known German pastor, Dietrich Bonhoeffer, who as early as the 1930s could clearly see clouds of Nazi persecution rising in his land, wrote:

By his enemies Jesus meant those who are quite intractable and utterly unresponsive to his love and who forgive us nothing, when we forgive them all.[43]

And then, when he had quoted that same verse which I have quoted in this paragraph, he added with both courage and conviction:

Love asks nothing in return but seeks out those who need it. And who needs our love more than those who are consumed with hatred and are utterly devoid of love? Who in the world deserves our love more than our enemy?[44]

A few years later Dietrich Bonhoeffer would be captured and imprisoned by the Nazis and in 1945 they executed him. His final letter, written to his family and friends, refers to his own inner peace and happiness.[45] And that, as he said, was a gift which came from deep within himself. It was the fruit of God's own Spirit working in his heart. It was a gift which even those who kill the body cannot take away! And yet, as all the psalm-beatitudes, those frequently recurring 'Ashray' verses,[46] make quite clear it is a gift which all who seek it, even if they are within a prison cell, are able to receive.

God

There was a practice in the early Church, among those people who used psalms for their own daily prayer, of having after each a period of silence. It gave them the time to think about the psalm which they had said and to reflect upon those verses which may have attracted their attention in a special way. It was as well, and even more importantly, the moment when the singer could be still and quiet in the awe-inspiring presence of the One to whom all prayer is offered but who is himself beyond what human words and even human thoughts are able to express or comprehend. Indeed God can be truly grasped, not by the brilliance of our human minds, but only by our love, as the author of the 'Cloud' declared.[47] And in the last analysis that love comes, not just from ourselves, but from the Spirit which is poured into our hearts and which then brings us, through the Son, into the mystery of the One who is, and will forever be.

Part Two

PSALM-VERSES VERSING US

Introduction

In this part I will concentrate on certain psalms and often just on single verses which have meant a lot to me and which I consequently would prefer not to omit. A number of them have been mentioned in the first part of this book but now the framework within which I use these psalms (or verses) and the way in which I use them will be somewhat different. They are arranged so that they form a certain sequence which should help the persons reading them to find an inner meaning to their lives and in that very process to be changed. I know that one could argue that this method introduces something which is not intrinsic to the psalms themselves but, since we have already introduced an extra element by saying that the psalms can be considered as the prayers of Christ, this further use does not seem to be a wrong or falsifying way to go. Indeed as I have tried to find and to respect the meaning which the psalmist of each psalm-verse had, to seek as well the meaning which it could have for all those who are the followers of Christ, and members of his body too, it appears to be a reasonable and, indeed, a very useful way of understanding them.

Texts for Prayerful Pondering

> O that today
> you would listen to his voice!
> 'Harden not your hearts as at Meribah,
> as on that day at Massah in the desert
> when your fathers put me to the test.'[1]

It was perhaps one of the temple prophets who first spoke these words! If so he would have said them to the people who had come into the Holy Place itself. And there, if we can take the first part of this psalm as evidence, they would have knelt and then bowed low before the One who made them and that unified prostration of so many must have been a most impressive sight indeed! And yet some kind of temple-prophet said to them that it was really not enough, that if they wanted to receive the blessings they required they must attend to what God wants to say to them as well. And, as the psalm-verse indicates, that meant a listening with the heart as well as with the head!

And Jesus, who was a prophetic figure too, said much the same! 'Listen to the word of God and do it,'[2] he proclaimed and, when he sensed that those to whom he spoke were hesitant, he urged them all the more and said, 'let those with ears to hear, now hear.'[3] And so we can accept the psalm-verse which I quoted as a psalm-verse which is being said to us by him, as well as by so many others from the past. Indeed, because there can so easily be 'Massah Moments' in our own lives too, that is occasions when we start to doubt that God is really good,[4] it can, indeed, be helpful for us to associate this invitation-verse with him who certainly did not allow his heart to grow insensitive and hard and who did learn to listen to his Father's wise and ever-guiding voice!

Indeed, the Liturgy itself quite frequently reminds us of this challenging and yet appealing line. It is part of a psalm which can be used to start the Church's Morning Prayer each day and which, until quite recently, was always the commencing, or invitatory, piece. As such, it seems to have impressed St Benedict who quoted it at the beginning of his Rule. 'O that today you would listen to his voice!' And so delighted was he with the fact that God should speak to him at all that he exclaimed: 'What can be sweeter to us, dearest brethren, than this voice of the Lord inviting us?'[5] Inviting us! Indeed, he knew, and from his own experience, that when God spoke it was, not just to give him practical advice on what to do, but also to invite him to come closer to himself!

> No speech, no word, no voice is heard
> yet their span extends to all the earth,
> their words to the utmost bounds
> of the world.[6]

To the utmost bounds of the world! It was to there that Jesus said his message was to go.[7] And so the Good News which he gave two thousand years ago has echoed down the centuries, and in so many lands, until today in our own land it has reached even us! And now as we accept and ponder it we too, as has been promised and as we are able to experience, can be set free, enlightened and transformed.[8] And then, through us, that message will be able to continue echoing and reach those generations which are still to come and places which await it even yet!

The psalm itself, or more precisely the first half of it, directs our gaze towards the starry 'heavens' and the 'firmament' above. And then it focuses our eyes upon the sun which every morning 'comes forth like a bridegroom from his tent', before it struggles with the darkness of the night which it of course inevitably overcomes. The second part speaks of the Law, or Word of God, and of how sweet and nourishing it is! It seems as if the psalmist wants to say that he who made the splendour of the sky can also, if we let him, make us splendid, too! And so, as we look up with admiration at what he has done, we can see signs of what we too can be!

The sun, which rises everyday made people such as St Augustine think especially of Christ who can enlighten everyone who comes into this world.[9] As for the firmament of shining stars they were, for him, the preachers and evangelists, who had absorbed the Word and who then preached the Good News to the world. 'It is they who proclaim to us the glory of God,'[10] he declared. Indeed the Liturgy itself, at least in Roman Catholic circles, often uses this same psalm when it desires to celebrate the feasts of the original apostles. But let us remember, too, those many others, some of whom we may have known and many who are nameless, but who all in their own ways have made it possible for God's Good News to reach our generation and ourselves. They, too, deserve a place among the stars!

A word, however, must be said about that special book, the Bible, which contains so much of the original and apostolic teaching of the Church and which makes it available to us. In it we can, indeed, discover many twinkling lights, like Matthew, Mark and Luke and John and Paul and all the others who, although from quite a distance, still can speak to us. There are, of course, a lot of other authors who in later times have passed this precious teaching on, and who are also 'stars', but this one volume does stand out as the essential core collection of the word 'whose span' the psalmist says 'extends to all the earth'. And so we find ourselves being challenged now to 'take and read' it, as, in his day, St Augustine was,[11] and, like him, to absorb its vital and life-giving Word. And as we do and as we now, in turn, 'take up the story'[12] which has been passed down to us we can, perhaps, accept the fact that we as well are called to be, at least for some, among those shining stars which may in fact effect the lives of generations yet to come!

If the Lord does not build the house
in vain do its builders labour.[13]

It is a kind of proverb really! And, let it be said, it would not be too difficult to think of some old temple sage repeating it to pilgrims if they came up and consulted him about their future plans. But other verses of this psalm, it could be mentioned here, have this same ring of wisdom-lore about them too. And yet as we possess them now they have become a part of temple worship and in such a situation are no doubt intended to evoke not only a response of natural appreciation for a saying which is wise but one of simple trust in God who can in all our undertakings help us too! It is, we know, the Lord who has to build the 'house', if it is to be satisfactory and good!

Perhaps the author of this verse was influenced by words which we can now read for ourselves in the Book of Deuteronomy.[14] In them a preacher is described as warning all the Israelites who were about to go into the Promised Land that building houses and increasing flocks and herds would not do them much good at all if, at the same time, they forgot the One to whom they owed so very much. Beware of saying: 'My own strength has won all this for me,' he said. And we could benefit, perhaps, from such a warning, too. Indeed St Benedict, who was himself a wisdom-figure, wrote in the beginning of the Prologue to his Rule that at the very start of any work we all should ask the Lord 'most

earnestly to bring it to perfection'.[15] Then, we will not only be
prepared to give God thanks when it is done but more disposed to
'build the kind of house' which he himself inspires.

We should, however, think a little more about this 'house'
which God desires to build. It is, in fact, not one of bricks at all
but one of living stones.[16] It is an active and supportive
fellowship, indeed a fellowship of friends, that God wants to
create and here I cannot help recalling Francis of Assisi who, as
everybody knows, came to appreciate this truth and in a very
special way. He heard a voice, so we are told, a voice which said
to him 'Repair my Church'. While he initially thought it was the
chapel of San Damiano, in which he was praying, that the Lord
desired him to repair he later on became aware that it was
Christendom itself! And so he started doing what he could to
counteract the unjust and divisive ways of his society and to
encourage everyone to share what they considered theirs and to
take special care of those who had the greatest need. And so, in
doing this, he grew himself to be a truly living stone and one
which could support a lot of others too. And us? Are we not called
to be, in our own different ways, such living stones as well?

But if we are to build this kind of 'house' and to continue
building it each day we will most certainly need all the help from
God that we can get. And so we must make time to listen to his
living and creative Word. We must be ready too to let his Spirit
enter into us. And so we need to plug in, as it were, through
prayer into the very source of power and life if he, the Lord, is to
become, through us, the architect and builder of this ever new
and 'spiritual house'. And then, when it is finished, or when even
some small part of it will be, if only for a little while, a welcoming
enclosure we may see, intuitively, that this 'house', this fellowship
of friends, is God's own dwelling place indeed, and that he
obviously is in residence as well!

Do not cast me away from your presence,
nor deprive me of your holy spirit.[17]

Prayer is important if we are to let this Spirit flow through us.
I do not just mean 'saying prayers', though that too has its place,

but being still and open to that presence which can enter into us and fill us with itself. For this no words are necessary (though a few may be of use), and thoughts as much as possible are better left aside. All that is really needed is just simply to 'be there' and gratefully aware that at that very moment we are being loved by God. And though at times that may not seem to be a prayer at all it is, and one which is extremely fruitful for it comes, not only from ourselves, but from the Spirit which is mingling with our own.

And yet that which is very simple can be difficult as well. There are so many things which press on us that, when we try to settle down for quiet prayer, a few of them at least will surely come and work their way into our minds and worry us until we find ourselves responding and then going off to do what in our hearts we know is not so urgent that it cannot wait. Or, we may feel that we just cannot cope with all the silence and the stillness and that consequently we, as quickly as is possible, must move and get away! But, maybe, at that very moment some small inner voice begins to whisper saying that we should resist what is but a temptation and remain. And so a person whom I knew said that, in such a situation, he would pray: 'Lord, do not let me go', 'Lord, keep me here', 'Lord, teach me how to stay.' But then, as he was ready to confess, such prayers were seldom of much use to him at all. In fact, if anything they tended only to make him more conscious of his tendency to go! And so, one day he turned his underlying thought around and, putting as it were the blame on God, said 'Lord, do not cast me away; O Lord: do not deprive me of your Holy Spirit.' And, as soon as he did that, he found that he became more conscious of his other and his deeper need, which was of course to stay!

It was, perhaps, a kind of game that he was playing but it was a game which many conscientious people find is often well worthwhile. As for the psalmist, who appears to have invented it – I say *appears*! – he was quite clearly very much aware of his own sinfulness and that itself may have suggested that he was not even worthy to remain. And we today can often feel that 'quiet prayer' is something, not for sinners like ourselves, but for such other people as the Poor Clares or the Carmelites or those who have been called by God to be what people call 'contemplatives'.

And yet those same contemplatives would be the very first to say that all of us, no matter who we are or what we may have done, should ask the Lord to fill us with his Spirit and then learn to wait, with confidence, for it will surely come. Indeed the very fact that we are sinners is another reason, and perhaps the best of all, for asking God 'not to deprive us of his holy Spirit' which of course is, as we know, the very thing that he would never even want to do!

> He will conceal you with his pinions
> and under his wings
> you will find refuge.[18]

Bird-life does not feature too much in the Scriptures! So to speak of God as having wings or pinions is a somewhat unexpected metaphor, though not an unappealing one, one must admit. In fact a number of the psalms refer to being in, or wanting to be in, the shadow of his wings[19] and in the book of Exodus we actually read that God, who rescued Moses and his followers from Egypt 'carried them on eagle's wings' and brought them, not just to a Promised Land, but to himself.[20] And so we have an image which expresses the desire and power of God to care for us but one which seems to hint at a maternal love as well. In fact did another and a greater Moses not echo this when speaking, not about an eagle but about an ordinary hen which gathers all her brood and brings them, with much more agitation than an eagle does, into a safer and more nourishing terrain?[21]

This image of a God who shelters and protects his people as with outstretched wings is able to create in us a certain feeling of security and of peace. Indeed the psalm itself, from which this one verse has been taken, is a very calming and consoling one. And for that reason it has been, for centuries indeed, a Compline or a Night Prayer psalm and for that bedtime hour it is a favourite with many to this day.[22] It is, indeed, worthwhile reflecting on. It is a psalm in which the God, whose wings surround us, seems to say, especially as darkness falls, that he will always care for us and that, no matter what may happen, all, with his help, will be well.

Jesus, too, knew this consoling psalm. And even if the verse which promises angelic help was able to suggest a reckless and an unwise thought, as the 'temptations in the desert' section of the gospels show,[23] he knew within himself how safe he really was and how completely he could trust his Father to protect him from all evil and all harm. Indeed the introduction of a verse about protecting angels only seems to strengthen the essential meaning of the psalm, for angels too were thought to have strong wings (and who am I to say that they do not?) And so the followers of Christ, the psalmist seems to say, need not have any fear for they are well protected and enfolded by that eagle's wings, and wings of angels too, suggest, that is the Spirit of the Living God himself.

Happy the man whose offence is forgiven.[24]

This is certainly one of the psalm-beatitudes. It is one of those 'ashrey' verses which I have already mentioned and which are so full of promise and appeal. But maybe I should offer some apology to readers here for, as I indicated in the Introduction, I am using the translation which is printed in the Prayer Book of the Church and this is one of those occasions where inclusive language could most certainly have been preferred. The word which is translated 'man' in Hebrew means a 'woman', too! Indeed to have such happiness as is implied, implies in turn the presence of the Spirit in our hearts, and that is something which is promised to us all! And everybody, therefore, male and female, can receive this calming and rejuvenating gift.

This 'happiness' of which the psalmist speaks, however, only came to him, as we can see, when he confessed whatever sin it was that worried him. And that, in his case, did not happen for a while for, as he tells us, he had kept his sin a secret and had been for much too long weighted down with misery and guilt. But then he found, it would appear, someone in whom he could confide and who in turn was able to assure him that the Lord had certainly forgiven him and that, no matter what he may have done, all would indeed be well. That person was most probably, I would suggest, one of those temple-prophets who appear, or half-appear, from time to time, as we have seen, within the psalms themselves.

But now, and thanks no doubt to him, the psalmist found that he was able to relax again and to discover that there was indeed a 'happiness' emerging from the depths within himself!

We should perhaps go back at this stage and reflect a little on a story which the psalmist surely must have known. It is the story of King David who confessed to Nathan (though in his case not until he had been challenged) and who was informed that, while the child whom he had fathered was about to die, God had in fact forgiven him.[25] Indeed the writer of this psalm, or maybe it was some collector after him, inscribed above it 'psalm of David' as a title for the benefit of those who would make use of it in later times.[26] Or we could go ahead and read the well-known story of the Prodigal Son in which the son who had spent all his money living in a sinful way decided to return to his own father's house, and did. And there he too, as we are told, was ready to confess.[27] The psalm could also be considered his! But if king David heard the prophet say that God had put his sin away the wastrel son discovered, through the warm and unexpected welcome he received, much more, much more indeed!

He found that, even though he had done so much wrong, his father did not speak one word of blame, much less of condemnation, when he finally returned. Instead he was embraced and fitted out with robes and rings and given, as we know, the place of honour at a banquet which was there and then prepared. The parable proclaims that God, despite our preconceptions, is in fact like that! He is the loving Father and, as people know, love is quite often in a strange way blind![28] That does not mean that we can just do what we like because we know that we will be forgiven in the end. But it does mean that we should never be afraid and that, when we have sinned, we can, with confidence, confess what we have done and know with certainty that, even if some people, when they hear, may not know how to cope, God always does and will. And then, despite our apprehensions, the beatitude which he has promised in the psalm-verse, I have quoted, will indeed be ours.

O Lord,
it is you who are my portion and cup.[29]

There were twelve tribes in Israel. And one of them, the Levites, was a little different from the rest. It was the priestly tribe, associated with the Ark and with the shrines, and with the worship of the God who had done so much for the people in the past. The Levites, therefore, were devoted to the Lord and in a very special way and so, according to an old tradition, were not even given, as were all the other tribes, a portion of the Holy Land to cultivate for their own daily needs. The Lord himself was their inheritance and 'portion' and on him they were expected to depend![30] That was a high ideal and a demanding one as well, but there are also statements which proclaim how happy (we have met the word before) the Levite dwelling in the house of God and dedicated to the Lord could actually be![31]

Is there in this a model for the Christian too? I think perhaps there is. Indeed when we take up the Gospels we discover Jesus saying to his own disciples that all those who leave their parents and their lands for his sake and the gospels' sake will certainly be blessed.[32] In the early Church the Christians who had been disowned by their own families, as many were, must have found consolation in his words and in the fruit of that inheritance or 'portion' which was theirs. Indeed I met not very long ago a lady in Nigeria who said that she was beaten (by her father) and rejected (by her brothers and her sisters) when she said that she would not do what they wanted her to do because she had decided to become a Christian and a follower of Christ! And there are many others in the history of the Church who, in their own lives, found that they too were forced to make this same most difficult decision. But, in this case, what impressed me most was the real happiness which that young lady obviously had, when, some weeks later, she was formally accepted by the members of the local Christian Church and solemnly baptised.

And Jesus too, who must have known and used this psalm, fits this same pattern as well. Do not the gospels say that in his public preaching life he frequently did not have any place where he could even lay his head?[33] And do they not say too that, even if his family did not officially disown him, they were not encouraging about the way that he behaved and sometimes even seem to have considered him abnormal or deranged.[34] He too, in his own way, had to let go of many things! And yet, if God was his inheritance and 'portion', in the 'cup' of blessings which he welcomed he was able to receive the inner strength and peace he needed to survive the separation from so many and so much. The 'cup' included sorrow but it was also a symbol of the joy which God alone can give and which, deep down in our own hearts, we all so much desire!

> You do not ask for sacrifice
> and offerings,
> but an open ear.
> You do not ask for holocaust
> and victim.
> Instead, here am I.[35]

This psalmist shows some temple-sacrifice antipathy! He is, it seems, in the tradition of the prophets who perceived how easy it can be to go through certain rituals and not be any closer at the end to God who wants in any case, not bulls and goats, but our own very selves.[36] He is in the tradition which declares that our obedience is better than a sacrifice[37] (although of course there can at times be quite a lot of sacrifice involved in that as well). Indeed the main thrust of this psalmist seems to be that of the 'servant' who, according to Isaiah, listened to the Lord and, in response, allowed himself to be the sacrificial lamb.[38] And so whatever was to happen in the temple after that could only be in some way an expression of the inner offering which was already made!

The writer of the Letter to the Hebrews must have heard this verse but, when he did, it obviously seemed to him that it was to the voice of Christ himself that he was listening. He knew that Jesus was himself a person who had listened and accepted in his heart the word of God. He knew that he was one who, though he had to learn it in the school of suffering, knew what it was to do the Father's will.[39] He knew that 'with loud cries and tears' he offered up himself in sacrifice to God.[40] And all that seemed to him to give a new and somewhat stunning meaning to this older yet prophetic verse. Indeed the fact that the translation, which the author of this letter had, said, not that God desired 'an open ear' but that he had prepared 'a body', which could then be offered as a sacrificial gift, made this verse even more prophetic of what later would take place on Calvary.[41] And so the writer of the letter to the Hebrews, and a line of preachers after him, found one more text which they could put into their teaching repertoire! And those who read and meditate upon this verse today find one, which does not only speak to them of Christ, but which perhaps can help them, too, to take their place in his all-satisfying sacrifice.[42]

'If when enemies set upon you (and) you persevere in the face of trials and (if) you want to learn the advantage of endurance' say this psalm, St Athanasius wrote to Marcellinus long ago.[43] But it, of course, was St Augustine who gave us the vision which allows us to perceive what praying this verse of this psalm implies. He said that in the 'body' which has been prepared we can perceive, not just the body which was on the cross, but that of the whole Church as well. And so the offering to God of that same 'body' is not just the offering which Jesus made of his own life at Calvary, important and unique though it most surely was, but the self-offering of many others too. And so it is the sacrificial offering of all of us, made in the Spirit to the Father[44] who of course, because he sees in us his own beloved Son, accepts us as we are and is prepared, through him, to raise us, like the 'servant' in Isaiah, 'very high'.[45]

The Lord's voice rending the oak tree
and stripping the forest bare.[46]

I was going to omit this psalm but felt on second thoughts that it would be a good idea to keep it and to use it at this point. I do because it is a psalm about a storm and it is frequently through some kind of a storm that God reveals himself to us. And so in this case what I would suggest is that you read not just the verse which I have quoted here but all the other verses of this psalm as well. But, when you do, allow its words to help you hear the storm 'resounding on the waters' and then 'shattering the trees' and then imagine all those sudden flashes which light up the sky and even seem to make the hills and mountains jump! And then note how all these phenomena are, by the psalmist, understood to be the voice of God himself! No doubt they told him something of his awe-inspiring power. But, if they did, they also symbolise for us those other 'storms' which we, no doubt, have known in our own lives and have, perhaps, already put behind us. But they symbolise as well that greatest 'storm' of all, the one which took place on the hill of Calvary!

The passion which took place in those last hours of Jesus was most certainly a 'storm'. It was, as we might say in this part of the world, the rending of the royal oak. And, since we too cannot escape the batterings of life we could say that the 'stripping of the forest' is itself a reference to us. But now I am indulging in a kind of allegory.[47] Yet it is an allegory which, perhaps, is quite acceptable for, as we know, there blows through all creation the destructive power of death! And so the 'Christ' must also die! The man from Galilee had to be led towards his cross and as he intimated we, who follow him, have to be led as well, and led to where so many of us, so often, do not want to go![48]

And yet the death which comes is not the end of everything but the beginning of a new and better life. The storm gives way to calm, the seeds of fallen trees produce new shoots which grow, and lightning flashes seem in retrospect to have revealed not only mountains jumping, as it were from fright, but joyful 'hills like yearling sheep'[49] foretelling the deliverance of something altogether new: a people who can find an unexpected freedom and a happiness which will not ever cease! And so the Christ is lifted up, and all of us who are his 'body' are a part of that rejuvenation, too.

This is my resting place for ever,
here have I chosen to live.[50]

The dwelling place of God on earth was, for the Jews, Jerusalem. There the sacred temple had been built and there, as we have seen, the Ark itself was kept. And so it was to Zion, or Jerusalem, that pilgrims came: to pray and to be still and to receive the blessings which flowed from the Presence which was there.

But now The Holy Place is not the city of Jerusalem, important though that city is. The Holy Place is now a person, that of Christ. He is, as he himself said to the Jews, the temple now.[51] He is the one in whom the fullness of the godhead dwells, as we read in the letter to Colossae.[52] So it is to him that we must go and then, through him, we will receive from God the blessings that we need.

But Christ is not just Jesus, who was born at Bethlehem and who some decades later preached the good news to the people of his time. Christ is as well each one of us. And so we are, as Paul wrote in his letter to the Church at Corinth, 'temples of the Holy Spirit' too![53] It is in us that God desires to dwell! Indeed to each of us he seems to say, 'You are my resting place forever; it is in yourself that I desire to be.'

We are the Holy Place. The sentence of St Paul, to which I have alluded, is most certainly a powerful one but sometimes I prefer to speak instead of 'tabernacles', which is a familiar word at least to Roman Catholics and to some Anglicans as well. And so adapting that verse in the letter to the Church at Corinth I could say: 'Do you not know that your own bodies are the tabernacles of the Holy Spirit?' There, within yourselves, in silence and with love you can discover him who wants to sanctify your lives and bless you more and more. And if we do go to the local church and sit before the tabernacle there, which is itself a worthy thing to do, let that not hinder us from recognising and respecting the Real Presence which is in ourselves and which desires to grow.

I thank you for the wonder of my being.[54]

Years ago a missionary sister working in Nairobi held a meeting in her house. When it was finished one of those who had been at it saw upon her desk a poster which displayed some sort of picture or design and under that the words which, as a title for this section, I have quoted. Could he have it? Sure! And so, quite happy with his unexpected acquisition, he went home! It was a year, perhaps, before they met again and this time it was for another meeting and a meeting which had been arranged to take place, not in her house, but in his. And there, when they had finished their discussions, she, the sister, asked if she could be 'excused'! Of course! So off she went. But when she closed the door and sat down on the toilet, there in front of her what did she see but that same poster with the thought-provoking words: 'I thank you, Lord, for the wonder of my being'!

Well, why not? It may not be exactly what the psalmist had in mind when he composed this psalm but did not God create our bodies too? And are they not in their own way, and in the way they work, quite wonderful? And so, when we reflect on it, do they not tell us something of the wisdom and the goodness of the One from whom, like all good things, they come? But let us move to what the psalmist really means. It is that he is quite delighted that the God from whom he tried so hard to flee has actually caught him and that, in the process, he had found that, deep down in himself, that was in fact what he had wanted all the time. How strange indeed the way that we are made! A part of us can be reluctant and obstreperous at times but somewhere in ourselves there is that other part which yearns for him from whom it comes and which, indeed, can even tame the 'outer and the wilder part' as well![55] 'I thank you, Lord, for the wonder of my being' sang the psalmist and there are, no doubt, occasions when we feel that we can do the same.

It is of course not only our own spirit which is seeking God but God's own Spirit in us mingling with our own. It is that Spirit which unites us with the Son and then, through him, to the eternal Father, from whom everything has come. And so each one of us, so wonderful in many ways, is also able to become a part of something which is much more wonderful than we can ever comprehend. And yet, despite the fact that there are aspects of ourselves which we may not admire, and they are only the not-yet-completed parts of the design, we are indeed already capable of entering into the very life of God himself. And so it is with deepest gratitude that we can make our own the psalmist's ancient prayer, 'I thank you, Lord, for the way that you have made me, and I thank you for the very wonder of my being.'

Visit this vine and protect it,
the vine your right hand has planted.[56]

The vine is one of those inclusive metaphors in Scripture which describe the chosen people as a whole! It was a 'vine', the psalmist says, which had been taken out of Egypt and which then was planted in a promised land so that it might spread out its branches far and wide, and even to the Tigris and Euphrates, those great mighty rivers in the east. That was, of course, more than the people ever managed to achieve; it was a dream and yet it was for them a dream which never went away. It was a dream which even grew with the conviction that the God they worshipped was a God of power and love who could and would do great and mighty things for them and, through them, for a lot of other people too. The vine which he had planted would, they knew, not only grow but, somehow, bear much fruit!

And yet of course that was the very thing which frequently it did not do. God did his best, he planted it and nourished it but, as one of the greatest of the prophets said, the only fruit it seemed to bear at times were wild and useless grapes.[57] And so, as if in punishment, invasions came and God's own vine was trampled down and sometimes all but totally destroyed. And yet each time, to quote that prophet once again, the stump remained[58] and in each generation it would stir itself and put forth new and energetic shoots. There was, despite their many weaknesses, a strong and indestructible desire within the chosen people to reach for the light and to produce those better grapes which would, apart from other things, make it attractive to the world around.

The vine, however, as we know, is really Christ. He is, the gospel of St John suggests,[59] the total plant of which we who accept him are the 'branches', as he said himself. And so it is his life which, like the sap within the vine, is flowing through ourselves as we remain in him. And as we celebrate with one another our 'companionship',[60] for this example of the vine is given in the context of a sacred meal, we should be able to help one another to grow strong and at the same time find the energy to spread out, not just to 'the River', but to every corner of the earth. And then, through us, the Spirit of the loving God will touch the yearning world and offer it as well the wine which it desires, the wine which cheers the heart[61] and which can always re-invigorate the human and the ever-thirsty soul.

A new song to the Lord.[62]

When Miriam, the prophetess, discovered that they all had crossed the sea and that they all were safe, she took a timbrel in her hand and danced and sang a song of gratitude to God.[63] And that was something which, in different ways, would be repeated many times throughout the years and centuries to come. And as I ventured to suggest, when speaking about praising God, it was a celebration which was somewhat archetypal too.

And so let us turn to the Book of Revelations, to that great apocalyptic vision of St John, for there we read that those who are beside the 'sea of glass' are holding harps and singing 'Great and wonderful are all your deeds O Lord.'[64] It is the 'new song' which all those who reach the final shore will sing. It is the song of Moses and it is the song of him who is referred to as the 'Lamb' for it is through the paschal sacrifice that he leads all of us, new Moses that he is, into the everlasting and completely satisfying promised land.

It is the song of praise which God himself has put into our hearts. It is the song which is, from all eternity, sung by the Spirit which, as I have frequently re-stated, mingles with our own. It is the song of Christ, our head, who now is raised on high. And so it is the song which God himself enjoys and which is able to become with him a single melody, now and for evermore.

Part Three

Damn Them All

I have already mentioned, although very briefly, that there are some less than Christlike verses in the psalms. Indeed there are a lot of downright curses and they can even be found in what could otherwise be thought of as respectable and proper prayers. The Roman Breviary, I know, omits the more offensive lines but those who use the psalter as it is are often quite surprised to find that they must wade through many verses which are filled with angry and revengeful thoughts. And then, of course, they wonder what to do with them and even if they should be read at all. And so perhaps an extra word of explanation might not go amiss.

But first let us survey a little of the scene. Let us take up the psalter and pick out the cursing-verses and examine them. They are, as we will see, against the 'evil-doers' of the day, although we could add 'evil-doers from the curser's point of view'! And so some are directed against people who made life a burden for the psalmist by the things they said and some refer to people doing things against him too. One psalmist, for example cries:

> Arise Lord; save me, my God,
> you who strike all my foes on the mouth,
> you who break the teeth of the wicked.[1]

While another, full of impotent frustration, prays:

> repay them as their actions deserve, …
> give them their deserts.[2]

And then, to take a third example here, there is the psalmist who appears to be as eloquent as he is angry and who solemnly declares:

let his children be fatherless orphans
and his wife become a widow …
Let the creditor seize all his goods.[3]

Wow! What can we do with such appalling lines? Are we to leave
them out or are we to pretend that they mean something else?
Perhaps are we simply to acknowledge them for what they are
and then to see how they can be incorporated into a design, or
pattern of growth, such as the one which I have painted in Part
One? This last course is, I think, the only honest one and in the
end the only satisfactory approach.

And so let me begin by making a suggestion: that these
vengeful thoughts and stinging words may have resulted from
the simple fact that there did not appear to be in those days
anyone who could cope with the 'evil-doers' except God! If, for
example, there had been a well-developed and a fair judiciary the
psalmist could have gone to the police and said that such and
such a person had offended him by word or deed or, failing that,
he could have gone to his solicitor and with the help of expert
lawyers fought his case in court. And then, if he was really in the
right, some other people would have done the dirty work and
put the guilty person into prison while the psalmist could have
quietly got on with his own spiritual life! But that was not the
case. There was no organised police force and, while there were
certainly some courts and judges, they, according to the prophets,
were quite often less than fair. And so the psalmist often had no
option but to call on God himself and hope that he would do what
his society could not.

That does make sense. But on the other hand we have to ask
how much can all those curses help us now when we sit down to
pray the psalms today. The world in which we live is different to
theirs. Unlike the psalmist we possess that luxury of picking up
a phone and of politely getting rid of those who otherwise could
make our lives unbearable. And yet, one could reply that all those
verses have a value for they show us how we might ourselves
behave if, for example, our society were to disintegrate or if we
felt that in some situation we were but the helpless victims of
injustice or discrimination of some kind. For then perhaps we,

too, would turn to God and beg him to get rid of those who were
upsetting us! And then perhaps, if things were really bad, a sense
of sheer frustration might oppress us and we, too, might find that
we did not have any option but to curse!

Meanwhile, however, and while grateful that our own lives at
the moment are secure, it could be useful for our reading of these
psalms to turn the television on and to observe the pictures of
those people who have to exist in lands where justice can be very
primitive indeed. Perhaps they feel a little as the psalmist did and,
though such people often have amazing patience, they must
surely feel at times the need to let a pent-up rage explode! And
those who are invaded by the armies of some other ethnic group,
and who have in the fighting lost their homes and many of their
families and friends, may often feel like shouting out to God in
desperation and, imploring him to come and drive their perse-
cuting enemies away.

> My God, scatter them like chaff,
> drive them like straw in the wind![4]

And like the Jews, who were defeated and then driven into exile
by the Babylonians, such people may at times not only wish their
persecutors dead but all those who belong to them as well.

> O Babylon, destroyer,
> he is happy who repays you
> the ills you brought on us.
> He shall seize and shall dash
> your children on the rock![5]

Yes, there is much anger and frustration there. But that is how
such people feel. And as we listen to them we, who may feel
mildly angry that such things can happen, have at least the
opportunity to sympathise with them who are, in fact, our
brothers and our sisters in this world, And, if we can do nothing
else, we can at least pray for their needs and for their badly
needed peace.

But still we have to ask, 'Is cursing, even when one is unfairly treated and upset, the right and only thing to do?' In asking that, however, we reveal that we have probably been influenced, not only by a life which makes recourse to cursing much less necessary, but by the example of the one who could forgive his enemies as well.[6] And so it would seem that the answer must be 'no, to curse is not the thing to do' and that, to answer here another question, 'it might be, indeed, a good idea to purify the psalms, at least by the deletion of the more offending lines'. And yet before we do that we should note that, while it certainly is possible to learn how to forgive the person who offends us and, indeed, to turn the other cheek,[7] an element of struggle still goes on. An 'enemy' remains! He may now seem to be a different kind of enemy but 'enemy' he is and he is somehow there and we must learn to recognise his tactics and, then, with the help of God, to keep him in control.

And even Jesus had to do the same. And so he battled with 'temptations' in his life.[8] He fought the 'powers of darkness' which he found and which, of course, can be discovered in us all. St Benedict, who knew this too, referred to that objectionable verse which speaks about the slaughtering of children on the rock and said that all those children were the evil thoughts which can invade our minds and which must be annihilated there and then before they have a chance to grow.[10] And we, who keep on trying to live good and Christlike lives, know too how difficult the struggle is at times. And so, while it may take some mental effort as we read the psalms to keep transferring all these curses from the person, or the persons, to whom they, at first, were targeted to the much less definable but real power of 'sin', it is, in fact, a valuable and important thing to do. We must, of course, respect the anguish of the psalmist, and of those who are like him today, but we must also see quite clearly where the battle really is!

Our Human Dignity

How great is your name, O Lord our God,
through all the earth!

Your majesty is praised above the heavens;
on the lips of children and of babes
you have found praise to foil your enemy,
to silence the foe and the rebel.

When I see the heavens,
the work of your hands,
the moon and the stars
which you arranged,
what is man
that you should keep him in mind,
mortal man that you care for him?

Yet you have made him
little less than a god;
with honour and glory you crowned him,
gave him power over the work of your hand,
put all things under his feet.

All of them, sheep and cattle,
yes, even the savage beasts,
birds of the air, and fish
that make their way through the waters.

How great is your name, O Lord our God,
through all the earth![1]

The book of Genesis tells us that, on the seventh day, God spoke
and humankind was made. Male and female he created them and
then, as we are also told, he gave them power to order and subdue

all things. 'And let them have dominion over the fish of the sea and over the birds of the air and over every creeping thing that creeps upon the earth.'[2] And day by day as we explore this planet and this universe of ours, our power and our dominion seem to grow. Indeed, at times, there is no limit visible to what we may achieve!

And yet, as we know too, we are in fact so small and almost insignificant! The psalmist recognised that when he stood and looked up at the stars! And we, who know that they are much more numerous and much more wonderful than he could ever have imagined, can be filled with even greater awe when we, in turn, gaze at that same amazing sky. And then, as we become aware that we are only floating on the fringe of what is but one cluster of a million stars and on what is, in fact, not much more than a little piece of rock, we can feel very small indeed, and in a strange way almost insecure! And with a new awareness then we too can ask that question which the psalmist has already asked: 'Lord, what are we at all that you, who are so great, should keep us all in mind?'

And Jesus may have felt the same. He too was born beneath that fascinating yet impenetrable sky. He too lived day-to-day within the confines of an ordinary human life. Indeed St Paul wrote in his letter to the Church at Philippi that he accepted his condition and did not consider an equality with God as something to be grasped![3] Of course, that could refer to his abasement in becoming human, to his letting go in some way of his own divine omnipotence, and it was in that sense of Incarnation that the author of the letter to the Hebrews understood the phrase 'a little less than god', or 'than the angels' as his version obviously said.[4] But it could also mean that Jesus, who was human, was content within himself and, irrespective of a previous existence, did not want to play at being god, as for example the first Adam did.[5] And that gives us a way of understanding this important verse so that we too can welcome our humanity and then give thanks to God who made us as we are.

But then God raised him up! 'With glory and honour' he was crowned! And there, no doubt, we glimpse the final answer to the question which the psalmist asked: why does he keep us all in mind? It is because we are a part of Christ. It is because he made us to participate in that life which is now forever his! And here I must apologise again for the defects of non-inclusive language but, although the English is at best ambiguous, the Hebrew and the Greek both use a word which means both man and woman too. And so we all are called to be divine, to be 'a little less than God' if I can use that phrase again and this time in a divinising way. We all are called to share that power which can, not only overcome all darkness and 'the savage beasts',[6] but is no less than God's own Spirit growing in our own! And so we all can know the One from whom it comes and, like the psalmist, have the privilege of glorifying him 'through all the earth', and then in that 'infinity' which is, as we believe, beyond!

ALL INTO ALL

In the beginning, we are told, the Spirit came and hovered over what the author of the book of Genesis imagined as confused and troubled water.[1] Then, when all was calm and still, God spoke and many things, as we are also told, were made, not least our very selves.[2] And so God in a new, and yet not altogether different way, was glorified!

That Spirit, as we know, must come to us as well if we are to allow the Word of God to enter into us, and then to make us, even slowly, into what we have been called to be. And so it is important to be still,[3] as one of the best-known of all the temple-prophets said to people who may have been agitated at the time. But it is equally important, too, to wait in patience,[4] as a psalmist, who appears to have been something of a sage, declared. And so, when we take up our psalter, we must learn to give the Spirit time to 'hover' over us and time to turn the soil of our own souls if, in the end, the psalm-words which we read are to take root in our own lives and then to blossom there.

The important thing during psalmody is to remain vulnerable before the psalm, ready to receive what its text and the operation of the Holy Spirit inspire.

So writes a modern monk.[5]

Of course one has to spend some time reflecting on the meaning of the different verses of the different psalms. That is the effort which we all must make and which, as those who make it know, is certainly worthwhile. It is the effort, too, to which the French Cistercian André Louf referred when, speaking of the psalms, he said:

anyone whose heart is not awakened must give his (or her) attention to the words and try to make them his (or her) own.[6]

This is, in fact, what Cardinal Hume as we have seen advised. And it, I hope, is what this book may help some of its readers to achieve. But then, when that is done, when God's own Spirit has shown us the meaning of the psalms, that Spirit will itself begin to pray more vigorously in our hearts and we will need just to attend to that. As André Louf continued:

> when the heart is already awakened he (or she) need only hear and listen to it. The words of the psalms speak to him (or her) of the movement of his (or her) own heart.[7]

And as we listen we ourselves will grow and then become the most important word, the word which is incarnate once again!

And so it is the Spirit which transforms us and, in helping us to understand and to receive the Word, unites us to the One from whom it comes. The thought of St Augustine then is true: God is the source as well as the conclusion of our prayer.

Ut bene ab hominibus laudetur
laudat se ipse Deus.[8]

God, in order that he might be truly praised by humankind, praises his own self. Or, if you would prefer, God through his Son (who is the Word) and therefore through the total Christ both gives and welcomes in the Spirit all the praise which he so much deserves.

And that, of course, is something which we will not ever fully comprehend for it is infinite! But it is what is happening as we pray the psalms and will for evermore!

NOTES

Introduction
1. *Searching for God* by Basil Cardinal Hume. Hodder & Stoughton, (1977) p. 51.
2. Most modern Bibles follow the Hebrew Bible enumeration of the psalms. Liturgical books on the other hand, at least in Roman Catholic circles, follow the Greek (the Septuagint) and Latin (Vulgate) numbering. Some Bibles, such as the Jerusalem Bible, offer both.

Part One
Essentials
1. 'Thirty Psalmists, Personalities in the Psalter' by James Fleming. N.Y. Seabury Press. 1945.
2. St Athanasius (*c.*297–373) was Bishop of Alexandria and Doctor of the Church. He wrote to Marcellinus who was one of the deacons in the local church and who, he heard, had taken up the psalms for private study while recovering from an illness.
3. Ps 22/23.
4. Ps 22/23.
5. Ps 89/90.
6. cf. Rom 8, 16.
7. cf. Ex 3, 1–4 'Yahweh' is translated generally as 'I am who am.' But sometimes a translator underlines an existential note and gives instead: 'I am who am for you.'
8. cf. Ex 3, 6.
9. Ps 98/99.
10. Ps 94/95.
11. Ps 144/145.
12. cf. J.D. Crichton: 'Christian Celebration: The Prayer of the Church', Chapman (1976), p. 85.
13. Arius (*c.*250–336) was a priest of Alexandria who preached that Christ was not divine. He was condemned at the Council of Nicea (325) but the reaction of the Church in emphasising the divinity of Christ had the inevitable result of underscoring his humanity. The same could be said about the 'Glory be' which is in use today.

People

1. cf. *The Psalms are our Prayer* by Albert Gelin, P.S.S., translated by Michael Bell and published by the Liturgical Press, Collegeville, Minnesota, 1964.

2. cf. 1 Sam 1 where we read that Elkanah and Anna went on pilgrimage to Shilo and psalm 77/78, v.60 which refers to the occasion when that shrine was both destroyed and then abandoned during the invasions of the Philistines (*c.*11th cent. BC).

3. cf. 2 Sam 6 which contains the story of how David brought the Ark to Zion, which would have been about the year 1,000 BC.

4. Ps 131/132.

5. Ps 14/15.

6. St Hilary (*c.*315–*c.*367) was the Bishop of Poitiers, in modern France, and a strong presence in the development of Church life in that place.

7. Ps 121/122.

8. The Law referred to the Ten Commandments, then to new collections which were formulated later. These are found today in certain chapters of the books of Exodus and Deuteronomy and in other parts of the Pentateuch (the first five books of the Old Testament). The Torah was the Hebrew word and had the connotation of a revelation given by the Lord and then communicated by the temple priests. But these words could be used as well in a much wider sense.

9. Joshua, who led the Israelites across the Jordan and into the Promised Land, was told by God, so we are told, to meditate upon the Law both day and night, which is not really what one would expect a warrior would do! cf. Jos. 1, 8.

10. Ps 1. The Jerusalem Bible reads: '… and murmurs his law day and night'.

11. Ps 18/19. It is possible but not certain that this psalm was composed as one poem by the one author. The first part praises God for the splendour of the skies, the second for what he can do in us through his all-powerful and appealing word.

12. Ps 118/119. This psalm is alphabetical, that is each section starts with a new letter of the Hebrew alphabet. Indeed each verse within each section starts with that same letter too.

13. Ps 118/119. v.105.

14. Ps 118/119. v.130.

15. Ps 118/119. v.10.

16. cf. Gen 41, 37–43 where Joseph is appointed by Pharaoh as chief administrator in the land. But note the comment made in Acts 7, 22 as well.

17. cf. 1 Kgs 5, 29–34.

18. The Greeks were great philosophers and, while the authors of the

books of Job and of Ecclesiastes challenged the accepted thought that those who do the will of God succeed, the author of the Book of Wisdom, influenced in Alexandria by Grecian and Platonic thought, discovered that he had good reason to believe in a new life to come where all who put their trust in God will be most certainly rewarded.

19. Ps 104/105.
20. cf. 1 Kgs 10.
21. Ps 31/32.
22. Ps 33/34.
23. Ps 36/37.
24. Ps 1.
25. Ps 72/73. This psalm has always been a favourite and manifests the struggle of the individual much more than many of the others do.
26. Ps 72/73.
27. Ps 72/73.
28. Ps 6.
29. Ps 27/28.
30. Ps 54/55.
31. cf. 1 Pet 5, 7.
32. St Basil (*c.*329–79) was Bishop of Caesarea in Cappadocia and is recognised as a Doctor of the Church.
33. Ps. 11/12.
34. Ps. 45/46.
35. cf. 1 Sam 8–12. Two accounts of Saul becoming king are interwoven in these chapters. One comes from those who were supporters of a royal and hereditary power. The other came from those who argued that an earthly monarch would impinge on God's supreme authority. This struggle and the subsequent anointing of a king took place in the 11th cent. BC.
36. cf. 2 Sam 7, 11–12. This is the famous statement of the prophet Nathan which was understood as giving to the House of David the divine approval which it claimed to have.
37. cf. 2 Kgs 25. The last few chapters of 2 Kings describe the final days and fall of Zion, which definitively took place in 587 BC.
38. Ps 77/78.
39. Ps 131/132.
40. Ps 88/89.
41. Ps 19/20.
42. Ps 19/20.
43. Ps 71/72.
44. Ps 71/72.

Life

1. Ps 62/63. This song is one of somebody who may have been a Jewish priest but who was certainly a person who found strength and consolation in the temple of Jerusalem.
2. Ps 113/115.
3. Ps 113/115.
4. Ps 62/63.
5. Ps 41/42. This prayer was one of somebody who used to lead the 'crowds into the house of God' and who now lets such memories sustain him in his exile while he obviously yearns for blessings still to come.
6. Ps 41/42.
7. Ps 41/42.
8. 'The Hound of Heaven', poem by Francis Thompson (1859–1907).
9. Ps 32/33.
10. Ps 30/31. cf. Pss 66/67; 79/80.
11. Ps 39/40.
12. cf. Rom 8, 16.
13. Ps 37/38.
14. Ps 34/35.
15. John Cassian (*c*.360–*c*.435) was a monk at Bethlehem who visited the old monastic settlements in Egypt and who travelled then to Rome and finally to Gaul where, near Marseilles, he founded two monastic houses: one for men and one for women. It was for the monks and nuns in them that he wrote down the doctrine which he had himself received from the Egyptian pioneers.
16. Ps 69/70 The version given in the text is that which is used in the Prayer Book of the Church. The one used in the Grail edition reads:

> O God, make haste to my rescue
> Lord, come to my aid.

The famous statement of John Cassian is that this verse is a 'formula, which the mind should unceasingly cling to until strengthened by the use of it and by continual meditation, it casts off and rejects the rich material of all manner of thoughts, and restricts itself to the poverty of this one verse'.
17. Ps 129/130. This 'de profundis' psalm is better known, perhaps, as one which finds a very fitting place in Christian-funeral liturgies.
18. Ps 122/123.
19. Ps 50/51. The Jews attributed this well-known penitential psalm to David. It expressed, they said, his sorrow and repentance when he was accused by Nathan of his sinning with Bethsheba. cf. 2 Sam 11–12.
20. *Rahamim* (compassion) comes from *Rehem* (the Hebrew word for a mother's womb).

21. Ps 50/51.
22. Ps 50/51.
23. Ps 50/51.
24. Ps 50/51.
25. Ps 32/33.
26. The Jewish community called the Book of Psalms the *Tehillim*, the hymns of praise. The word 'psalm' comes from the Greek 'psalmos' which derives from 'Psalterion' meaning a stringed instrument, such as a harp. The *Tehillim*, of course, included, not just lamentations and thanksgiving psalms but other types as well, such as the wisdom or didactic ones (e.g. Pss 1; 18b/19b; 118/119).
27. In the Jewish Haggadah we find the following exhortation: 'In every generation one must so regard oneself as if he too (or she) were coming out of Egypt.'
28. Ps 135/136.
29. Ps 135/136.
30. Ps 33/34.
31. Ps 91/92.
32. Ps 91/92.
33. Ps 150.
34. cf. Ex 15, 20–1.
35. Ps 103/104.
36. Ps 148.
37. It may be interesting to note that in the Roman Catholic liturgy and in the 4th Eucharistic Prayer we find the following text:

> In the name of every creature under heaven
> we too praise your glory as we sing/say.
> Holy, holy, holy, etc.

38. cf. 1 Pet 4, 11. This phrase was quoted by St Benedict in his Rule and has become one of the 'mottos' of his Order ever since.

Living Signs
1 Ps 76/77.
2 Ps 77/78.
3 Ps 27/28.
4. Ezechiel, who preached before and during the great Exile (AD 587–37) castigated those last kings who had been false and selfish shepherds and declared that God himself would be the people's shepherd now. The famous chapter is Ez 34.
5. Ps 22/23.

6. Ps 22/23.

7. cf. Rev 7, 13–17.

8. Ps 22/23.

9. Ps 22/23 The psalmist seems to look around him and to see with gratitude the temple liturgy and those who, with anointed heads (cf. Ps 44/45), are sharing joyfully in it. God is a gracious host as well as a protective shepherd on this journey throughout life. Indeed there even seems to be in this last verse some real anticipation of that happiness which we associate with that life which is yet to come.

10. Ps 109/110.

11. Apart from Samuel, who was an unenthusiastic champion of the king, there was, before him, Gideon whose famous statement sums up well the anti-monarchy position (cf. Jud 8, 23).

12. Ps 98/99.

13. Ps 92/93.

14. cf. Ex 19, 16–20.

15. Ps 96/97.

16. Ps 96/97.

17. Ps 97/98.

18. Ps 97/98.

19. Pss 95/96, 97/98.

20. Ps 130/131.

21. Ps 130/131.

22. cf. Isa 49, 15.

23. Julian of Norwich, the 14th-century anchorite, wrote in her *Revelations of Divine Love*:

> as truly as God is our father, so truly is God our mother

and, a little later on:

> our courteous mother … wants us to behave like a child. For
> when it is distressed, it runs quickly
> to its mother …
> (Colledge & Walsh translation: SPCK London)

24. The Rock, according to the Book of Exodus, chapter 17, gushed forth a stream of water to refresh the people on their journey to the Promised Land. A later Jewish legend stated that that rock accompanied the people from that moment as they travelled on! And that allowed St Paul to see in it a symbol of the one who now sustains us all, the Christ. cf. 1 Cor 10, 4.

25. Ps 17/18.

26. cf. 2 Kgs 19, 32–5.

27. Ps 90/91.

28. cf. Zach 2, 5.

29. A similar metaphor is found in Ps 124/125:

Jerusalem! The mountains surround her,
so the Lord surrounds his people
both now and for ever.

30. cf. 1 Kgs 18, 41–5.
31. Ps 64/65.
32. Ps 103/104.
33. cf. Isa 8, 5–8.
34. Ps 45/46.
35. Eccl 15, 3.
36. Ps 35/36.
37. cf. Ex 13, 21–2.
38. Ps 26/27.
39. Ps 42/43. NB. This psalm is considered to be a continuation of the previous one. Because of the line:

I will come to the altar of God,

it was used until the Vatican II reforms as the opening and preparatory prayer for the Roman Catholic Mass.
40. Ps 89/90.
41. Ps 56/57.
42. cf. 2 Kgs 19, 35.
43. Ps 29/30.
44. Many people point to the 2nd century (BC) Book of Wisdom as the first real indication of belief in an afterlife (cf. especially Wis. 3).
45. Dahood, in the Anchor Bible argues for this earlier awareness of an afterlife.
46. Ps 26/27.

Trinity
1. cf. Heb 4, 15.
2. cf. Acts 2, 24. The earlier statements say that God (the Father) raised up Jesus from the dead; St John, whose gospel comes from a later date, says that he had himself the power to lay down his own life and then to take it up again (cf. Jn 10, 17).
3. cf. Lk 9, 51.
4. cf. Jn 14, 2.
5. For one example cf. Lk 4, 18–19. But many people would suggest that Jesus found in Scripture the Isaian references to the so-called 'suffering servant' (cf. Isa 52, 13–53, 12 et al.) and the reference in Daniel to the Son

of Man (Dan 7, 13–14) and that he managed, quite uniquely to identify with both.

6. cf. Jn 4, 19.

7. Ps 15/16.

8. In the Roman Catholic liturgy this psalm has an honoured place on Holy Saturday, that day of calm expectancy.

9. Ps 2.

10. cf. Acts 13, 32–3.

11. Ps 109/110.

12. Ps 109/110.

13. cf. Gen 14, 18–20.

14. cf. Heb 5, 1–6; 7, 1–3.

15. cf. Heb 7, 25.

16. *Aislinge Meic Conglinne* ('The Vision of Mac Conglinne') is a satire on the Irish Church, written about the year 1,100. cf. 'The Psalter in early Irish Monastic Spirituality' by Martin McNamara in *Monastic Studies*, Advent 1983.

17. Ps 21/22.

18. Ps 21/22.

19. Ps 21/22.

20. Other psalms, and verses, which in the New Testament are understood as having some Last Supper or some Passion Narrative pre-reference would include

a) Ps 40/41 which seems to speak of Judas:

> Thus even my friend, in whom I trusted,
> who ate my bread, has turned against me.

b) Ps 2 which seems to speak of the new-found friendship between Pontius Pilate and King Herod as they both contributed to the rejection and the execution of the one who certainly considered 'the poor and the weak':

> They arise, the kings of the earth,
> princes plot against the Lord and his
> anointed (cf. Acts 2, 24–27; Lk 23, 12).

c) Ps 68/69 which seems to be the words of Christ himself as he was hanging on the cross:

> For food they gave me poison; in my thirst they gave me vinegar
> to drink.

This psalm was also used in connection with the cleansing of the temple episode. cf. v.10 and Jn 2, 17.

d) Ps 30/31 which seems to give us those words which were said by Jesus, and by Stephen too, as he was just about to breath his last:

Into your hands I commend my spirit.

21. St Ambrose (*c.*339–79), from whose writings this quotation has been taken, was the Bishop of Milan and is recognised as one of the Doctors of the Church.

22. Ps 2.

23. Ps 117/118. The verse which 'need not concern us here' is that which speaks about the stone which the builders rejected. It is referred to in Mt 21, 42; Acts 4, 11 and 1 Pet 2, 7.

24. The Hallel psalms: Ps 135/136 was called the Great Hallel; the other one, the one referred to here, is in fact a group of psalms: Pss 112/113–117/118.

This latter Hallel was the one used by the Jews in the celebration of their Passover meal.

25. Ps 117/118.

26. Ps 117/118.

27. Ps 117/118.

28. Another psalm which could be mentioned here is that one which the Liturgy has taken for its celebration of the feast of the Ascension. Originally it referred to the procession of the Ark into Jerusalem (cf. 2 Sam 6) but now it indicates the entrance into heaven of the Son of Man.

God goes up with shouts of joy
the Lord goes up with trumpet blast.
(Ps 46. cf. Ps 23, 7–10)

29. cf. *Aislinge Meic Conglinne.*

30. cf. Acts 16, 25.

31. cf. Jas 5, 13.

32. 'The Priest Rediscovers His Psalm-Book', translated by Frank O'Connor (Penguin Books, 1981).

33. St Columba (*c.*521–597) was an Irish monk who founded a well-known and influential monastery on the island of Iona.

34. St Augustine (354–430) was Bishop of Hippo in the North of Africa.

35. Ibid.

36. cf. Gen 1, 2. *Tohubohu* was the empty and formless mass on which the Spirit had to hover so that it could be responsive to the Word of God. We need the Spirit too if God's creative Word is to become effective in ourselves.

37. St Basil. P. G., 29, 211–14.

38. cf. Gen 1, 26–7. God created in his image humankind, both male and female, and he blessed them. But creation only reaches its perfection in the person of Jesus Christ, according to Col 1, 15.

39. Ps 132 / 133.

40. St Basil, loc. cit.

41. St Hildegarde of Bingen writing to the Bishop of Mainz who had put her convent under interdict because she had agreed to the burial of an excommunicated nobleman (1178).

42. Ps 108 / 109.

43. *The Cost of Discipleship* by Dietrich Bonhoeffer, SCM Press (1959), p. 132–3.

44. Ibid.

45. *Letters & Papers from Prison* by Deitrich Bonhoeffer, Macmillan Publishing Co. Inc., N.Y. 1973.

46. 'Ashray' is the Hebrew word for 'Happiness' or maybe more correctly for 'Oh, the happiness of ...' Sometimes of course 'blessed' is used instead. In the psalms there are a number of 'Ashray' verses or beatitudes, for example:

> Blessed are they who put their trust in God. (Ps 2)
> Happy the man whose offence is forgiven. (Ps 31 / 32)
> They are happy whose God is the Lord. (Ps 32 / 33)
> Happy the man who considers the poor and the weak. (Ps 40 / 41)
> They are happy who dwell in your house (Ps 83 / 84)
> Happy the man whom you teach, O Lord. (Ps 93 / 94)

47. *The Cloud of Unknowing* by an anonymous 14th-century English writer.

Praying the Psalms to Christ.

Jesus is also Lord, according to St Paul. And so the psalms can be addressed to him. This is, in fact, a way of praying psalms which has a long tradition in the Church, and some psalms lend themselves to it in a very special way. For example, the Good Shepherd psalm (22/23) is almost difficult to say without remembering how Christ, according to St John, attributed that title to himself. The problem, if there is one, is that such a method which inevitably emphasises the divinity of Christ may, if we use it frequently, reduce our sensitivity to his humanity and all that it, in his particular case, implies: namely his high priestly role and mediatorship. And yet St John, who certainly does not deny his very real humanity, does say that those who see him see the Father too!

Part Two

1. Ps 94/95 Meribah and Massah both refer to that place in the desert where the Israelites complained because there seemed to be no water there to drink. The passage in the Book of Exodus deserves to be well read. cf. Ex, 17, 1–7.

2 Lk 8, 21.

3. cf. Mt 3, 9, 17, 43.

4. We could say that the complaining of the Israelites resulted from the fact that they did not completely trust the Lord and that that, according to the psalmist, was because they did not really listen to his voice.

5. *Rule of St Benedict*, Prologue (6th cent.) translated by Abbot Justin McCann and published by Burns Oates (1952).

6. Ps 18/19.

7. Acts 1, 8; Mt 28, 19.

8. Jn 1, 9, 12.

9. St Augustine in his commentary on Psalm 18 wrote:

> When the word was made flesh he found, as a bridegroom, his nuptial chamber in the virgin's womb. There he came forth, united to a human nature.

(*Ancient Christian Writers* series. The Newman Press, London, 1960)

10. St Augustine, op. cit.

11. 'Take and Read.' These are the words which St Augustine heard when he was still deliberating as to what he ought to do. And so he went back to the place where he had been and, from the table that was there, took up the Scriptures, opened them and read. And thereupon all darkness vanished and his heart was filled with light.

12. Ps 18/19.

13. Ps 126/127.

14. Deut 8, 11–20.

15. *Rule of St Benedict*, Prologue. RB 1980 edition. Published by The Liturgical Press, Collegeville, Minnesota. 1981.

16. 1 Pet 2, 5.

17. Ps 50/51.

18. Ps 90/91.

19. cf. Pss 16/35/56/60/62/90.

20. Ex 19, 4; Deut 32, 11.

21. Lk 13, 34–5.

22. The modern Roman Breviary allots this psalm to Night Prayer (Compline) every Sunday; the Monastic office keeps the older custom of reciting it each night.

23. Mt 4, 5. Satan, we are told, quotes this psalm to entice the Son of God to be imprudent but his misinterpretation of the passage is rejected.

24. Ps 31/32.

25. 2 Sam 12, 13–14. The story of king David sinning with Bathsheba is recounted in 2 Sam 11, 12.

26. Psalms of David. Many of the psalms have been explicitly attributed to David and a number do, in fact, suggest events in his own life. And then, to some extent because he was a harpist, he became the patron of them all. This made it easier, of course, for Christians, who believed that Jesus was the most important and the central singer of the psalms, to see them all in some way representing him.

27. Lk 15, 11–32. There is an oral tradition of this parable which tells us that the father hung a lamp outside his door and kept it lighting there in case his son should come back when he was himself elsewhere. And so that light was lighting even when the son was squandering his life and giving not a thought to him to whom he owed so much.

28. Julian of Norwich wrote that even our own sins do not stop God from loving us (*Revelations of Divine Love*, chapter 39).

29. Ps 15/16.

30. Deut 18, 1–2; Num 18, 20.

31. Ps 83/84.

32. Lk 10, 29–30.

33. Lk 9, 58.

34. Mt 3, 21:31–5; Jn 7, 5.

35. Ps 39/40.

36. cf. Ps 49/50. vv. 8–15.

37. cf. 1 Sam 15, 22; Mt 12, 7.

38. cf. Isa 49, 1; 53, 7.

39. Heb 5, 8.

40. Heb 5, 7.

41. Heb 10, 4–10. The Hebrew Bible was translated into Greek for those Jews living then in Gentile lands. This version, known since as the Septuagint, was used by the early Christian writers too for they, as well, were writing for those living in Greek-speaking lands. And sometimes, as in this case here, the version in the Septuagint provided thoughts which Christian writers found were very suitable to illustrate the message which they preached.

42. Col 1, 24. The letter to the Hebrews makes it very clear that Christ himself had offered for all time the one and perfect sacrifice. And yet the author of this letter to Colossae wrote:

> I rejoice in all my sufferings, and in my flesh I now complete what is lacking in his afflictions …

43. St Athanasius, *Letter to Marcellinus*.

44. cf. Heb 9, 14.

45. Isa 52, 13.

46. Ps 28/29.

47. An allegory is a literary composition in which every detail is considered to refer to some reality. It would, of course, be much too complicated to use in a normal sermon but it could be used, and often was, in commentaries on the parables which had themselves been preached. At times, of course, it could become exaggerated and, in fact, tell us much more about the writer's mind than about the text itself.

48. Jn 21, 18.

49. cf. Ps 113/114. This verse (and the first part of this psalm), commemorates, in a poetic and a joyful way, the great event which had occurred when God brought out his people from their slavery in Egypt.

50. Ps 131/132.

51. Jn 2, 19–21.

52. Col 1, 19; 2, 9.

53. 1 Cor 3, 16; 6, 19.

54. Ps 138/139.

55. cf. Julian of Norwich, *Revelations of Divine Love*, Chapter 19.

56. Ps 79/80.

57. Isa 5, 1–2.

58. Isa 6, 13.

59. Jn 15, 1–11.

60. 'Companion' comes from two words, both of which are Latin: *cum* meaning 'with' and *panis* meaning 'bread'. So 'companion' means a person with whom we are able to break bread!

61. cf. Ps 103/104 v.15.

62. Ps 95/96; 97/98.

63. Ex 15, 20–1.

64. Rev 15, 2–4.

Part Three
Damn Them All

1. Ps 3.

2. Ps 27/28.

3. Ps 108/109.

4. Ps 82/83.

5. Ps 136/137.

6. cf. Lk 22, 34.

7. Mt 5, 39.

8. Mt 4, 1–11; Heb 5, 15.

9. *Rule of Benedict*, Prologue.

Our Human Dignity
1. Ps 8.
2. Gen 1, 26-28.
3. Phil 2, 6.
4. Heb 2, 5–9.
5. Gen 3, 5.
6. cf. Mk 1, 13.

All in All
1. Gen 1, 2.
2. Gen 1, 26.
3. Ps 45/46.
4. Ps 36/37.
5. Michael Casey OCSO, *The Power of Psalmody, Cistercian Studies.* Vol. XVIII (1983) 2, p. 117.
6. Ardr Louf, *The Cistercian Alternative*, translated by Nivard Kinsella O.Cist. Gill and Macmillan (1983), pp. 98–9. Words in brackets mine.
7. Ibid.
8. St Augustine, *Commentary on Psalm 144.*